The Biblical Seminar
37

PAINFULLY CLEAR

PAINFULLY CLEAR

THE PARABLES OF JESUS

Andrew Parker

Sheffield Academic Press

To Barbara Parker who handed on to me the embers she had received.

To Roland Walls who fanned these into a flame.

To George Velten who drew me into the Mission Populaire.

Copyright © 1996 Sheffield Academic Press

Published by Sheffield Academic Press Ltd
Mansion House
19 Kingfield Road
Sheffield S11 9AS
England

Typeset by Sheffield Academic Press
and
Printed on acid-free paper in Great Britain
by Cromwell Press
Melksham, Wiltshire

British Library Cataloguing in Publication Data

A catalogue record for this book is available
from the British Library

ISBN 1-85075-771-2

CONTENTS

PREFACE

It is generally recognized that biblical commentaries are ideologically coloured. It is for this reason that we label their authors liberals, conservatives or radicals. However, the position one occupies in society is probably even more crucial than one's political leanings, in determining the way in which one writes. For example parish ministers sometimes criticize the work of academic biblicists as scarcely relevant to the concerns of ordinary Christians.

I am happy to admit that this book has been fundamentally shaped by my experience of looking at life from the standpoint of an unskilled manual worker. I made the decision to earn my living in this way some twenty-five years ago, in great trepidation. I badly wanted to be involved in 'spreading the news' but others had, in the meantime, brought me to see that this entailed paying more than just the usual lip service to the Bible's central bias for the poor.

Nevertheless, I would not want my book to be judged by anything other than the highest academic standards. For the rest, it is up to the reader to decide whether its peculiar shaping enlightens or clouds the words and work of Jesus.

Anyone who has dealt with the synoptic Gospels and has struggled with the problem of the underlying traditions and sources will be aware of the difficulty of saying anything about the authorship of a particular phrase without grossly over-simplifying what to all intents and purposes was an extremely complex development. However, in trying to allow for this complexity it is all too easy to end up with something that is quite unreadable. So I propose the following simplifications. If I suggest that Luke was responsible for some particular material or bias the reader must understand that I do not necessarily mean Luke himself but simply someone in the tradition that culminated in what we know as Luke's Gospel. In other words I shall use the names of the evangelists to indicate traditions rather than individuals. In the same vein I often use the term 'the early church' to mean the whole complex of traditions which culminated in the synoptic Gospels.

This book is a joint creation, for although the crude ideas that form its basis are entirely mine, a good friend, John Rowe, was equally involved with me in crafting them into their present form, taking into account the criticisms and suggestions of an even wider circle of friends, notably Ed Kessler and Jack Rowe.

If such teamwork has proved possible it is because John Rowe, an Anglican worker priest now retired, shares my basic standpoint. It may also be that the dialectic between his catholic (and English) adherence and my protestant (and Scottish) bias has had some effect on the final product!

That said I am very aware that had we been left to our own devices it is unlikely that these ideas would ever have entered into print. In this regard I would like to acknowledge the tolerant help offered by two university academics: Liz Templeton and Leslie Houlden. Without their criticism and encouragement we might have been left struggling with an unpublishable work.

Part I

Chapter 1

MODELS AND DEFINITIONS

From very early on in the Christian tradition the parables of Jesus have been seen as something of an enigma. While as stories they appear simple enough for a child to understand, working out what they actually mean is another matter.[1] The Gospels themselves draw attention to the problem. According to St Mark, when Jesus told the parable of The Sower to the crowd by the shore of lake Gennesaret the disciples asked him privately afterwards to explain to them how parables were to be understood (4.2-10). St Matthew reports both this conversation (13.10) and a similar one about the parable of The Weeds Among the Wheat (13.36). He also claims Jesus explained to the disciples, unasked, the meaning of the parable of The Drag-Net (13.47), and then checked with them afterwards to make sure they understood.

This initial problem of the *message* of the parables is closely associated with a second, the *mechanism*: how do they work and what is achieved by using a parable instead of more straightforward communication? Two of the sayings recorded in Mark have always been considered crucial in this regard:

> And he said to them, 'To you has been given the secret of the Kindom of God, but to those outside everything is in parables; so that they may indeed see but not perceive, and may indeed hear but not understand; lest they should turn again, and be forgiven.' (Mk 4.11, 12)

> With many such parables he spoke the word to them, as they were able to hear it; he did not speak to them without a parable, but privately to his own disciples he explained everything. (Mk 4.33, 34)

---

1. 'The hearers find themselves in a familiar scene where everything is so simple and clear that a child can understand... Nevertheless, the parables confront us with the difficult problem of recovering their original meaning', J. Jeremias, *The Parables of Jesus* (London: SCM Press, rev. edn, 1972), p. 12.

These texts appear to indicate that Jesus was delivering a series of teachings in a hidden manner. The obvious allegorical elements in many of Mark's parables gave early Christian interpreters the clue as to how this had been achieved. Jesus must have been using parables as *coded messages*, clear to some and obscure to others.

It was not until the end of the nineteenth century that a radical break was made with this general approach. Adolf Julicher had come to the conclusion that the evangelists' attempts to understand Jesus' stories allegorically were inappropriate, having the effect of weakening their pointed, true-to-life characteristics. He therefore employed a new model, treating Jesus as a teacher who employed parables as pedagogical tools to impart general moral and religious principles to simple peasants.[2] I call this hypothesis the *general illustration* model.

In 1935 C.H. Dodd criticized Julicher's new approach. While giving credit to him for exposing the fundamental flaw in the allegorical method of interpretation he went on to draw attention to the great defect of the general illustration model, pointing out that by envisaging Jesus as setting out 'the great enduring commonplaces of morals and religion' the parables' effects were greatly dulled and flattened.[3]

Dodd argued that to retain the true vitality of the parables it was essential to interpret them in the context of the historical crisis which Jesus' presence and activity was bringing about. He therefore suggested that Jesus used strange and vivid stories in order to arrest peoples' attention while keeping them in sufficient doubt about his precise intentions as to tease their minds into active thought.[4] I call this the *riddle* model.

Meanwhile, the German form critics were looking at parables from a rather different angle. Their interest was in comparing the different structural forms apparent in any given New Testament passage, including parable, with those of comparable non-biblical texts—from the Rabbinic traditions or Hellenistic folklore, for example—in order to trace the provenance and historicity of the passages in question. When it came to dealing with what I like to call the 'two-dimensional' sayings of Jesus—that is to say, logia in which he makes reference to one set of

---

2.   This is a summary of Dodd's and Jeremias's understanding of Julicher's model. See C.H. Dodd, *The Parables of the Kingdom* (London: Collins, rev. edn, 1961), pp. 22-23 and Jeremias, *Parables*, p. 19.

3.   Dodd, *Kingdom*, p. 22.

4.,   Dodd, *Kingdom*, p. 16.

circumstances in order to say something indirectly about another—
Rudolph Bultmann, the most influential of the form critics, attempted to
classify such sayings as hyperbole, paradox, metaphor, similitude,
exemplary story and parable. He thus made it clear that he believed a
distinction could be made between parable and other speech-forms.[5]

In 1947 Jeremias, while reaffirming and extending Dodd's work,
found fault with the form critics' understanding of parable as an
identifiable speech-form in itself.[6] It is not difficult to understand why.
For if you examine the whole range of Jesus' parables, as presented by
the evangelists, you find that while some of them look like coded messages others appear to be more like illustrations and others like
examples, and so forth, so that, try as you will, it seems quite impossible
to find one form into which they all fit.

Jeremias argued that parable is not the name for a precise speech-
form—like simile, metaphor, example, illustration—but an inclusive term
that can embrace all of these and many more. Jeremias thereby provided
what for many people has been a satisfying scholarly basis for this 'hold-
all' view of parable. He made the following points:

1. That the Aramaic word *mathla* translated as parable in the
    New Testament can mean parable but it can also mean simili-
    tude, allegory, fable, proverb, apocalyptic revelation, riddle and
    many other things besides.
2. That *mathla*, in Jesus' saying given in Mk 4.11, should have
    been translated as 'riddle', for the logion to have the required
    antithesis: 'To you the secret is revealed; those outside are
    confronted by riddles!'[7]
3. That Mark's understanding of parables as allegories, coded
    messages containing secret meanings hidden from outsiders, is
    the result of his mistakenly narrow use of *mathla* in this and
    other logia.

According to Jeremias, everything becomes clear if we see Mk 4.11-12
as an independent logion inserted between vv. 10 and 13 and as actually
a comment by Jesus on the nature of his teaching in general, not as a

5.   R. Bultmann, *The History of the Synoptic Tradition* (Oxford: Basil
Blackwell, 1963), pp. 166-178.
6.   Jeremias, *Parables*, p. 20.
7.   Jeremias, *Parables*, p. 16.

specific reference to his use of parables. In other words, Jesus was simply making the point that while his words were clear enough to his followers, they nonetheless remained a puzzle to outsiders. Viewed in this light, there would no longer be any reason to suppose that Jesus' parables were more hidden or secretive than his other teachings.[8] The conclusion by inference is that if the form critics came to grief it was because their search for forms led them to force Jesus' sayings 'into the categories of Greek rhetoric', when they should really have seen them in the broad sense of *mathla*.[9]

Jeremias never broached the question of the parabolic mechanism, presumably because it would have meant reintroducing the idea of the single parable form. However, there is evidence that he found this a difficult position to sustain since at one point he came close to hypothesizing a new model: 'For the most part, though not exclusively, they [the parables] are weapons of controversy.'[10]

The next significant contribution to the parable debate was made by Ernst Fuchs—the father of the 'new hermeneutic'—who succeeded Bultmann, his teacher, to the New Testament chair at Marburg University.[11] Bultmann had dealt with parables as part of his overall 'demythologizing' of the teaching of Jesus in the Gospels. In this his aim had been to bridge the gulf between the unacceptable, because outdated, language of the New Testament and the scientifically expressed concerns of modern technological humanity. He achieved this by a hermeneutical method in which the pre-scientific 'mythical' language operative on one side of the divide was translated into existential language on the other.

Adopting this approach Bultmann had treated language forms simply as vehicles for transmitting an understanding of existence and so, at the end of the day, as dispensable. Fuchs declared that this was wrong. He believed the language of the Gospel has to be considered not as a vehicle but as an event which brings into being something that was not there before the words were spoken. For him the parables were not existential meaning clothed in a discardable story form but a *verbalization of*

8.   Jeremias, *Parables*, p. 18.

9.   Jeremias, *Parables*, p. 20.

10. Jeremias, *Parables*, p. 21.

11. For my understanding of the 'new hermeneutic' school of interpretation I am indebted to N. Perrin and his excellent book *Jesus and the Language of the Kingdom: Symbol and Metaphor in New Testament Interpretation* (Philadelphia: Fortress Press, 1976).

Jesus' own existence, put on offer in such a way that his hearers could choose to share in his self-understanding.[12] In this way Fuchs directed attention to the fact that a parable's meaning cannot be abstracted from its story and reclothed or handled separately without the loss of something essential. The reason for this, as I see it, is that like all illustrations the parable delivers its illumination with a thrust developed from the illustrative material itself, so that if the story is discarded the parable's overall impact is lost as well.

But it is doubtful whether Fuchs would have agreed with this explanation, for all who have followed him in the new hermeneutic have made it clear that they see parables not as illustrations designed to illuminate outside referents but as *creative works of art* that fix attention upon themselves and have no need of outside references at all. I have to say that I fundamentally take issue with the new hermeneutic as regards this new model. As I see it, parables are emphatically not 'creative works' or 'art'. To say this is not to demean them nor to deny the exquisiteness of Jesus' stories; it is preparatory to suggesting that they have a more crucial, down-to-earth purpose.[13]

One way of resolving this argument would be to look at the inner workings of parable to see whether it possesses a mechanism capable of doing what Fuchs claims for it, bringing into existence something new and verbalizing Jesus' existence so that others can take on his self-understanding.[14] (Is there anyone, apart from Fuchs, who can see Jesus' stories as directly concerned with his self-understanding?)

However, Fuchs only discussed the parabolic mechanism in the simplest terms. He referred to parables as similitudes and constantly talked

12. See Perrin, quoting Fuchs: '... in the parables Jesus' understanding of his situation "enters language" in a special way', *Jesus*, p. 110.

13. I find it perfectly justifiable to talk about parables as 'creating awareness' so long as it is understood that this does not signify a bringing into being of something new but rather an opening of the eyes to what already exists; see Chapter 4, p. 63 below. As I see it the only legitimate way to use the word 'creative' in connection with Jesus' parables is to highlight the fact that as acts of healing they opened the door to renewed life and health in the situation—but this is to anticipate; see p. 71 below.

14. I make a distinction between the parable form and the parable mechanism, between the dead shape of a logion as it lies on the page and its animated shape when in use. The form is like the description one would give of a worker's tool one had never come across before and the mechanism is like the description one would give of the same tool after seeing it being used.

about the *tertium comparationis*,[15] thereby showing that he saw the phenomenon as the setting of two comparable entities side by side. It is interesting that though he spoke of parable as *sermon*, functioning as 'proclamation',[16] this indicates little that is significant about the way he thought the medium functions save, by implication, to indicate that it traffics in rational argument.

The hallmark of the new hermeneutic has been this ability to home in on important characteristics of the parable medium while at the same time strangely ignoring the way in which these features are developed by the mechanism itself. For example, Eberhard Jungel made the important observation that it was an error to treat parables as rational arguments. However, instead of showing how a rational approach contradicts some intrinsic feature of the parabolic mechanism, he was content simply to point out that it was at variance with the fundamental insight of the new hermeneutic: that parable is concerned with 'the disclosure of ultimacy'.[17]

This unwillingness to deal with the parable mechanism continued even after the new hermeneutic crossed the Atlantic. Amos Wilder, from the standpoint of a literary critic as well as a scholar of the New Testament, gave the impression that he was intent on dealing with the nuts-and-bolts issue when he stated that, whereas in simile the less known is clarified by the better known, in metaphor (under which category he considers parable) 'we have an image with a certain shock to the imagination which directly conveys [a] vision of what is signified'.[18] However, when you look at his argument carefully you see that it too amounts to nothing more than an unsubstantiated restatement of the basic thesis that parables are non-referential, creative works:

> Now we know that a true metaphor or symbol is more than a sign, it is a bearer of the reality to which it refers. The hearer not only learns about that reality, he participates in it. He is invaded by it. Here lies the power and fatefulness of art. Jesus' speech had the character not of instruction and ideas but of compelling imagination, of spell, of mythical shock and transformation.[19]

15. See Perrin, *Jesus*, p. 112.

16. E. Fuchs, *Studies of the Historical Jesus* (London: SCM Press; Nashville: Alec R. Allenson, 1964), p. 8 and pp. 19-28.

17. See Perrin, *Jesus*, p. 123.

18. A.N. Wilder, *The Language of the Gospel: Early Christian Rhetoric* (New York: Harper & Row, 1964), p. 80.

19. Wilder, *Language*, p. 92.

It is amazing that Wilder can suggest it is this distinction between creative work and referential illustration that separates metaphor from simile. If someone were to call me 'an old woman' I might legitimately accuse him of sexism and agism but hardly of being an artist, since his clear intention would have been to refer me to a feature in my behaviour. Of course it will be said that Wilder is not attempting to define how similes and metaphors actually work but to highlight the intrinsic difference between referential and non-referential techniques.[20] But this only further emphasizes my point: that like his predecessors in the new hermeneutic, Wilder refuses to take the mechanics of such speech-forms seriously, including that of parable.

This said, one clear advantage of Wilder's parable-as-art model is that it takes on board Jungel's realization that Jesus' stories were not rational arguments.[21] This model was later refined by Robert Funk and John Dominic Crossan who talked more precisely about Jesus' parable-making in terms of *poetic metaphor*.[22] On a purely technical level this model is unconvincing, since parables operate quite differently from metaphors, as we will discover in Chapter 4. Furthermore, when Jesus used metaphor it was to play upon the grotesqueness of a comparison and not to use its creative aspect to offer some radically new insight, as we will see in Chapter 2. To describe parables as art is hardly to recommend them as powerfully controversial language events. The world does not crucify someone for being creative.[23]

In any case, it is not helpful to describe Jesus' parables as poetry, wonderfully told as they certainly are. Even as they appear in the Bible a child (as I was when I first became fascinated by them) can appreciate their intense, single-minded illustrative character. The trouble is that they also appear strangely enigmatic because they often seem either to illuminate nothing very clearly or else to make rather mundane, not to say moralistic, points. My conclusion is that they are illuminative illustrations which have somehow lost their referents, not artistic stories that never

---

20. Wilder, *Language*, p. 80 n.2.

21. Wilder, *Language*, pp. 87-88.

22. R.W. Funk, *Language, Hermeneutic and the Word of God: The Problem of Language in the New Testament and Contemporary Theology* (New York: Harper & Row, 1966), p. 139; and J.D. Crossan, *In Parables: The Challenge of the Historical Jesus* (New York: Harper & Row, 1973), pp. 10-16.

23. See Chapter 5, pp. 103-104 below, for a fuller discussion of the hostility aroused by Jesus' parable-making.

had any. That said, we should take seriously what Amos Wilder says, for he brings to light important features of the parable that will require explanation when we come to examine the mechanism ourselves: for example, the shock involved in the parable approach and the sensation of participation that it brings about in the hearer.

Robert Funk also makes as if to analyse the mechanics of the parable medium without actually doing so. He draws a distinction between simile (A is like B) and metaphor (A is B) and states that, whereas in the former the element of comparison is illustrative, in the latter it is creative of meaning.[24] Here again is the new hermenutic's parable-as-art thesis in the guise of an analytical description of the working of the medium. The statement 'the element of comparison is illustrative' constitutes a fair summary of the mechanism of simile, but to say that 'the element of comparison is creative of meaning' is a far from adequate description of the workings of metaphor. In fact this latter statement appears to me to be itself metaphoric rather than analytic. The suggestion seems to be that Funk's 'metaphor' possesses in itself—quite independent of the person who speaks it—a special, indeed almost human, quality since only living beings are capable of creative activity. However, it turns out that all Funk means is that 'metaphor' possesses an openness which enables hearers to participate and bring along not just their rational faculties but their experience, including their emotional reactions as well. But this does not move the argument forward since the same openness and participation is present to a degree in all illustrations, even in the most mundane simile.

Funk makes it clear that he does not use the words simile and metaphor in a formal but in some other, 'substantive', sense[25] but this does not help. If the distinction he is talking about is real then it has to be marked by some characteristic of form or use. If this characteristic is not the formal one he himself has introduced, between 'A is like B' and 'A is B', then why has he introduced it? If some metaphors are, in his terms, 'simile' and some similes 'metaphor' then what other distinction marks the difference he is striving to pinpoint? To put the matter simply, if Funk's suggestion is that certain speech-forms, which for convenience he labels 'metaphor', induce hearers to participate then it behoves him to precisely identify the mechanism shared by these forms which calls forth this response.

24. Funk, *Hermeneutic*, p. 137.
25. Funk, *Hermeneutic*, p. 136 n.15.

This mystification is worsened when Funk introduces into the discussion a third form: the symbol. He claims that simile (A is like B), metaphor (A is B) and symbol (B represents A) are all comparisons and that symbolism is just metaphor with the primary term suppressed.[26] In this way he allows himself the option of envisaging parable not just as metaphor but as symbol as well. But this is disingenuous.

In the first place it is false to say that a symbol is a comparison, for whereas some symbols evidence an appropriateness between themselves and the objects they signify others do not.[27] Furthermore it is never a comparison of the two that constitutes the basic object of the exercise but the replacement, for some good reason, of the one by the other. This means that it is false to suggest, as Funk does, that a symbol is a type of metaphor. In fact a proper examination of their structure shows that the two forms are not just distinct but incompatible, as I shall demonstrate later.

This willingness to confuse metaphor and symbol explains why Funk is happy to use the 'riddle' model alongside his 'poetic metaphor' thesis.[28] He approves Dodd's contention that parable 'leaves the mind in sufficient doubt about its precise application to tease the mind into active thought' to explain what he calls its open-endedness.[29] He argues that the parable is only closed when the listener is drawn into it as participant.[30] He believes parable should be regarded as open-ended as far as potentiality for meaning is concerned, because to ascribe a particular application to a parable is to close off the possibility of the hearer's participation in the parable itself. In other words just as works of art are properly appreciated differently by different people so a parable should be seen as having many different possible meanings even to its first hearers.

My own thesis is that this involves a serious misconception for, as I shall show, when a parable is first expounded its thrust is both precise and painfully clear, leaving no doubt at all as to its objective. Nevertheless, Funk is surely right to suggest that (in a way he has failed to identify accurately) parables are participative and open-ended. So I shall

26. Funk, *Hermeneutic*, p. 137.

27. See Chapter 2 below, p. 32, 'the names we give our children'.

28. Cf. Wilder, *Language*, pp. 82-83, and D.O. Via, *The Parables: Their Literary and Existential Dimensions* (Philadelphia: Fortress Press, 1967), p. 10.

29. Funk, *Hermeneutic*, p. 133.

30. Funk, *Hermeneutic*, p. 143.

account for these characteristics when I come to examine the parable mechanism in Chapter 4.

Dan Otto Via was the next to make a significant contribution to the parable debate. In laying out his argument for the new hermeneutic he made four basic criticisms of what he termed 'the severely historical approach' as proposed by Dodd and Jeremias:

1. The non-biographical nature of the Gospels makes it difficult and dangerous to pinpoint the precise application of the parables.
2. The severely historical approach ignores the broad element of basic humanity in the parables.
3. The historical approach threatens to leave the parables speaking to their past historical situation but with nothing to say to the present.
4. The severely historical approach ignores the aesthetic nature and function of the parables.[31]

Taking Via's first two points: I believe he has done a service in reminding us of the real difficulties in reconstructing the parables and of the danger of taking these reconstructions too seriously when we do. However, this does not undermine my contention that each parable should be seen as having been delivered on a precise occasion as a response to something that had been said or done. We should guard against loosely interpreting them, as people often have, in the light of some supposed general state of affairs.

Further to this, experience has taught me that I can only hope to produce a credible reconstruction of a parable of Jesus when I am prepared to implicate myself by digging over my own experiences, thus allowing the parables to criticize my personal blindnesses. Perhaps Via is recognizing something of this in his third point.

But it is in Via's final point, which goes beyond anything that has been recognized by previous interpreters of the parables, where I find his insight and blindness most excruciatingly combined. He claims that when interpreting a parable one has to take the text seriously on its own terms. This means treating it as an aesthetic object in which all the elements are seen as relating to each other, the structure of their connections and relationships being determined by the author's creative composition.[32]

31. Via, *Parables*, pp. 21-24.
32. Via, *Parables*, pp. 73-76.

Via is right to say that a parable should be seen as all of a piece, each element playing its part in relating to the whole. He is therefore to be applauded when he insists that in the first instance a parable should be understood from out of this general coherent pattern of connections rather than from any supposed historical context. I refer to this same aspect of parables when I insist on the need to concentrate from the outset on what Dodd called *the logic of the story*.[33]

However, Via is surely going too far when he understands parables as essentially aesthetic objects. That is simply restating the 'creative art' thesis. He argues that like plays, paintings and music, parables are non-referential in that they do not point beyond themselves to something else, but create an experience in which attention is totally engaged by and riveted on the object itself. As I shall show, nothing could be further from the truth. At the moment of an encounter something has occurred which incites the parable-maker to direct the interlocutor's attention to a blindness from which he suffers. The parable is used precisely to make this reference.[34]

John Dominic Crossan is the scholar who has brought the new hermeneutic's understanding of parable as 'non-referential creative art' to its climax. After criticizing Jeremias's tentative 'weapons of controversy' comparison he puts forward his own musical model. According to this we are supposed to see Jesus as creating through his parables a stupendous religious symphony (my word) so as to enable his disciples to participate in his personal religious experience of God's intervention in human history. Within this overall whole, certain 'key' or 'paradigmatic' stories are heard as 'overtures', containing 'in themselves the entire parabolic melody'.[35] However, the mass of parables are understood as falling into groups (Advent, Reversal and Action) containing themes which first introduce and then counter and correct each other, thereby creating an appropriate 'linguistic eschatology'.[36]

How does this music model square with the memory of Jesus as parable-maker contained in the Gospels? If one sets aside the long discourses—since the evangelists seem to have constructed these by stringing together a large number of logia which they had in their possession, including many parabolic sayings—the picture presented in the

33. See Chapter 4 below, pp. 60-61.
34. See Chapter 6 below, pp. 108-109.
35. Crossan, *In Parables*, p. 33.
36. Crossan, *In Parables*, p. 119.

Gospels is of a man in his everyday contacts using stories quite spontaneously to reply to opponents' questions, criticisms and jibes. (The word 'opponent' is used loosely since it can include even Jesus' closest disciples.) Indeed there is something of a throw-away style about Jesus as parable-maker, since the object of the exercise is clearly not to involve opponents in a lengthy argument but to pull them up short and then to pass on, leaving them to their own devices.

This of course is the complete reverse of the picture presented by the music model. This dictates that parables should be 'read together'. One therefore tends to see them as being directed at initiates since only people who were constantly with Jesus would have been in a position to engage in such an activity. Moreover, the musical analogy forcibly inclines one to see parables as stories told in quiet surroundings, withdrawn from the distracting hustle and bustle of everyday life, since these are the conditions conducive to thoughtful religious experiences in which people can ponder and discuss at length on a chosen topic.

Bernard Brandon Scott is the most recent scholar in the new hermeneutic to advance the debate.[37] He is not uncritical of his predecessors in the the movement and describes as naive and romantic Funk's claims that parable as poetic metaphor is capable of a direct apprehension of reality and that parable and allegory are sharply distinct.[38] Scott believes that the debate as to whether parables are allegories is beside the point. What really matters is what he terms 'the direction of transference':

> Does the transference go from parable to referent or the other way? Does the referent determine the understanding of the parable? To put it even more boldly, is the parable a true illustration or is it dictated by what it illustrates? Even more, is parable an ornament or does it have cognitive value?[39]

37. This is a personal judgment. There are many scholars to choose from: for example H. Weder who in *Die Gleichnisse Jesus als Metaphern* (Gottingen: Vandenhoeck & Ruprecht, 1978), has, as it were, returned the new hermeneutic to Europe; or C.W. Hedrick, *Parables as Poetic Fictions: The Creative Voice of Jesus* (Peabody, MA: Hendrickson, 1995). It is not my intention to deal exhaustively with the work of this school but to set out what I judge to be the significant contributions which they make to an understanding of the form and function of the parables.

38. B.B. Scott, *Hear then a Parable: A Commentary on the Parables* (Philadelphia: Fortress Press, 1989), pp. 46-47. The debate as to whether parables are allegories is beside the point here. What really matters is what he terms 'the direction of transference'.

39. Scott, *Hear Then*, p. 47.

He gives his own answer to this question:

> As fictional redescriptions, parables demand that the primary direction of
> transference be from parable to referent, because the description exposes
> something new, not simply copying the already known.[40]

But there is nothing very new here for what he presents us with is
simply a rather more restrained definition of the parable-as-creative-art
thesis. The fact that he accepts this basic principle explains his espousal
of Via's notion that parables are aesthetic objects,[41] his rejection of
Jeremias's search for the parables' *Sitz im Leben* and his agreement
with I.A. Richards, that it is superstitious to believe that every parable
has a single proper meaning.[42]

Furthermore Scott demonstrates the typical unwillingness of the new
hermeneutic to analyse the parabolic mechanism. He tries to make a distinction between 'a true illustration' and 'one that is dictated by what it
illustrates', but, I must insist, in so far as an illustration cuts itself free
from its referent it ceases to be an illustration and becomes something
else. So Scott's 'true illustration', which I suppose one has to understand
as pure creative art, turns out to be no illustration at all. Like those who
preceded him in the new hermeneutic, Scott shares the guilt of mystify-
ing the parabolic mechanism by describing it in arty, literary terms.

Scott takes Jesus' parables to be fictional redescriptions of the
'Kingdom of God'[43] and sees them as maintaining some of the recognized currency of this first-century symbol but, more importantly, of
challenging and 'disordering' it as well.[44] He is not the originator of this
latter notion, which goes back at least as far as Wilder, but in his
approach it appears dominant.

On a technical level, I find it as arbitrary for Scott to argue that the
general referent of Jesus' parables was the Kingdom of God as it was
for Fuchs to argue that it was Jesus' self-understanding.[45] However, in
comparison with previous new-hermeneutic models the disordering idea
does recognize a robust quality in the parables which gives credence to

40. Scott, *Hear Then*, p. 48.
41. Scott, *Hear Then*, p. 41.
42. Scott, *Hear Then*, p. 45.
43. 'Jesus' parables are laid beside the kingdom of God... The parable is about
the kingdom, whether the connection is immediate or implied.' Scott, *Hear Then*,
p. 420.
44. Scott, *Hear Then*, pp. 39, 61-62.
45. See p. 14 above.

the evangelists' contention that it was because of some characteristic in Jesus' approach, particularly evident in his parables and healings, that the authorities within the community took great exception to him.[46]

That said, it is disappointing to turn and look at what Scott produces in his analyses of the individual parables. I had expected him to identify some sense of disturbing power and unsilenceable acuteness. Instead he paints pictures of a storyteller who went around surreptitiously and inferentially pulling peoples' cultural presuppositions from under them. Though a little cheeky this is hardly the sort of behaviour that would have provoked the authorities into getting rid of Jesus altogether.

In sketching thus far the development from Jeremias to Scott I have been concerned with the fruits of liberal scholarship. It has to be said that conservative theologians have generally remained unimpressed by these. As Craig Blomberg has shown in *Interpreting the Parables* their approach has been to maintain an allegorical understanding of Jesus' stories even while abandoning the grosser excesses denounced by Julicher. In other words they have continued to see 'speaking in parables' as a form of concealment in which the truth is hidden even as it is revealed: Jesus being the shepherd who provides leadership yet leaves people with space to make their own personal commitment.

Craig Blomberg gives his version of this concealment hypothesis by likening the parable to the novel: in this model Jesus is seen as communicating his message to his hearers only gradually.[47] As I shall be dealing quite fully with Blomberg's contribution in Chapter 5 I shall content myself here with saying that I find no mechanism within parable capable of performing this gradually revealing function.

In the mid-eighties John Drury gave a fresh twist to the renewed interest in allegory as an essential ingredient of the New Testament parables. Picking up a point first noted by followers of the new hermeneutic he argued that the reconstruction approach adopted by the major interpreters of parables since Julicher is fatally flawed because we do not possess any single indisputable authentic parable of Jesus to guide us.[48]

46. See Chapter 5, pp. 103-104 below, for a fuller discussion of the hostility aroused by Jesus' parable-making.

47. C.L. Blomberg, *Interpreting the Parables* (Leicester: Apollos, 1990), pp. 54-55.

48. J. Drury, *The Parables in the Gospels: History and Allegory* (London: SPCK, 1985), pp. 2-3.

For Drury the search for Jesus' original parables is a fruitless exercise because though they may indeed have existed they are now beyond recall. Thus instead of trying to abstract Jesus' authentic parables by, as it were, 'emptying them out of the evangelists books' he believes we should try 'to establish the functions of parables by reference to the tendencies of the books they are in'.[49] It is the evangelists' parables that we should be interested in, not the hypothetical ones of Jesus.

Notice that Drury puts the word 'function' in the plural. This is because he rightly recognises that each evangelist freely developed the parable approach in his own way. He argues that *Mark*, as the earliest, took as his basic model the bizarre and surreal allegorical *meshalim* found in the Hebrew Bible, especially in Ezekiel, adding his own touch of mystery by presenting them as unexplained riddles since in the main he interjected his parables without clearly indicating the subjects they addressed or providing interpretive solutions in the usual way.

On the other hand Drury sees *Matthew* as moving slightly away from the Ezekiel tradition, his model being something more like that on which the rabbinic parables were based. He writes that Matthew uses his parables not in order to dwell like Mark on the mystery of the kingdom but to 'elucidate and clarify' the allegories (and his parables are if anything more allegorical than Mark's), these being transparent.

For Drury, finally, *Luke* is the evangelist most removed from the Ezekiel tradition: 'the apocalyptic interpretation recedes (not to disappear, however) and...humane realism...takes over'.[50] The important thing to notice here is that Drury sees the strong realism and relative lack of allegory in the parables of the third Gospel as evidence of Luke's editorial work and not, as has sometimes been thought, of the presence of unadulterated parables of Jesus.

I have some sympathy with Drury's basic position. I too have noticed the circularity of argument in the reconstructionists' work which results from their attempts to abstract new theological meaning from their reconstructed parables. It is painfully obvious that all they finish with in this way is the theology with which they started out. They are like a

---

49. Drury, *Parables*, p. 1. Drury was not the first to analyse the parables in terms of each Gospel-author: M.D. Goulder had already begun this in 'Characteristics of the Parables in the Several Gospels', *JTS* 19.1, April 1968 and also in ch. 3 of his *Midrash and Lection in Matthew* (London: SPCK, 1974).

50. J. Drury, 'Parable', in R.J. Coggin and J.L. Houlden (eds.), *A Dictionary of Biblical Interpretation* (London: SCM Press, 1990), p. 511.

crooked paeleontologist who plants evidence in the ground and then shouts 'Eureka!' when later he digs it up. This fault is most conspicuous when we find them sorting out Jesus' parables into groups. Thus Dodd divides them into Parables of Crisis and Parables of Growth; Crossan uses a threefold division: Parables of Advent, Parables of Reversal and Parables of Action; whereas Jeremias has ten different categories.[51] Since there is no agreement about the number and content of the categories put forward, it is only too evident that such divisions arise from theological presuppositions rather than from intrinsic characteristics of the parables themselves.

It needs to be acknowledged that in using the parables to build a theology, if you come up with some idea not already found in the rest of the tradition it will have come from yourself and will not therefore be adequately attested. On the other hand if you introduce a teaching that is authentically attributable to Jesus it will be because you have brought it in from elsewhere in the tradition. This being the case it would be far better to discuss such teachings in their original contexts rather than in connection with the parables. In other words, reconstructionists like myself should refrain from categorizing the parables according to their supposed *meaning* since such classification will inevitably say more about our own theology than about the intentions of the parable-maker.[52] This is why I have been careful to number Jesus' stories according to strict rules based on the order in which they appear in the Gospels,[53] and why I have strenuously resisted the temptation to find theological patterns within them.

But if Drury is right to insist that reconstructed parables can reveal nothing we do not already know about Jesus' teaching it does not necessarily follow that, as he thinks, we are therefore delivered up to the tender mercies of the evangelists' freewheeling reconstructions, without any hope of approximating to what Jesus himself intended. He seems to have failed to take account of two considerations. The first is that in so far as the evangelists believed Jesus' parables dealt in theological teaching they were mistaken. Had they been right then we would indeed have

51. Dodd, *Kingdom*, chs. 5–6; Jeremias, *Parables*, ch. 3; Crossan, *In Parables*, chs. 2–4.

52. Scott is also aware of this danger. He writes: 'The various organisational plans, by subordinating the parables to some scheme outside the parable, view the individual parable from the perspective of the scheme.' *Hear Then*, p. 73.

53. See catalogue at end of Part I, pp. 117-21. below.

nowhere to go to avoid their errors. Happily, however, there are clear indications that this was not the case, as will be seen when I come to discuss my own model. The second consideration Drury ignores is that insofar as the evangelists understood Jesus' parables in terms of Ezekiel's allegorical *meshalim* they were led astray. As I will show in Chapter 4, the structure of Jesus' stories (the fact that each is constructed as a package of self-authenticating 'logic') not only radically distinguishes them from Ezekiel's *meshalim* but militates against their having been originally allegorical. The point is that any symbolic reference such a story might have contained would inevitably have distracted attention from the thrust generated by its 'logic', rendering the exercise as a whole counterproductive. (This was not a problem in the case of Ezekiel's meshalim since, having no self-authenticating 'logic' to spoil, they could be filled with symbolic references with impunity). Hence we cannot follow the evangelists in their allegorical reconstructions without manifestly betraying the intention of the parable-maker. This is especially true where, as is so often the case, the story's logic and the allegorical meaning intended by the evangelists go in different directions.

In short, while I believe that any parabolic reconstructions that I produce can reveal nothing new concerning Jesus' teaching I believe they can at the very least restore a proper understanding of *what Jesus was doing* when he told parables and this of itself is theologically relevant. In other words, if I reconstruct Jesus' parables it is to justify my model and not because, like some archaeologist, I hope to find a new body of information that has up to now lain hidden. In this respect I agree with those who say that one cannot get behind the evangelists. If I dare to break with these and follow where the stories themselves lead it is to rectify the evangelists' mistaken picture of Jesus the parable-maker as 'a teacher of wisdom' rather than try to search for some as yet unplumbed depth in his teaching.

Since all the above hypotheses are fundamentally flawed I have felt obliged to continue the quest for the parabolic model. I believe I have found one that convinces. I call it the *healing model* and the purpose of this book is to unveil it. I am aware how much it owes to the insights of others. However, as their inspiration sprang in large part from their recognition of the mistakes made by their predecessors, let me end this chapter by summarizing my basic criticisms of those whose ideas are generally reckoned to hold the field at the present time.

1.   Just as Julicher increased our understanding but did not take his criticism far enough, by highlighting the inadequacy of the allegorical method; so did Dodd, in claiming that Jesus' parables should be interpreted in the light of a particular application. So although Dodd was perfectly right to point out that each synoptic parable had arisen within a particular situation Jesus had encountered, he did not realize the need to associate each one of them with *a specific problem of awareness which Jesus can be seen to have identified in his interlocutor as a result of its manifesting itself in a particular incident.*

2.   Contrary to what Jeremias and the hold-all theorists maintain, I believe Jesus' original parables displayed the same form and general characteristics of usage as certain stories found elsewhere within Israel's tradition. It was only later that this was obscured by the way in which they were reported. Indeed, many of the stories of the rabbis in the Talmud and Midrashim (composed during the early Christian centuries) and even those used in a comparable culture today[54] demonstrate the same general workings. So we can only hope to come near to what Jesus intended if we first come to grips with this basic *mechanism*—something which liberals have failed to do satisfactorily and conservative scholars have preferred to avoid.

3.   Though it may be technically correct to label parables 'language events', as does the new hermeneutic—since the object of parables is to force the hearers, whether they like it or not, to open their eyes to reality rather than to offer them a rational explanation of it[55]—this is not to equate parables with 'creative language', such as the words used by the God 'who speaks and it is done'.[56] *Parable is most definitely a referential speech-form.* Therefore to treat Jesus' stories as creative art is to mystify their workings and obscure their nature.

4.   In spite of what Mark seems to have believed and many conservative scholars think, it is wrong to suggest that the type of parable Jesus used is a speech-form of concealment. A proper understanding of its mechanism shows that its function is to make some misunderstood reality *painfully clear.*

54. See below, p. 29.

55. This should not be taken as the new hermeneutic's own understanding of 'language event' but only as an indication of the extent to which I am prepared to go along with it.

56. See Wilder, *Language*, pp. 14-15.

Chapter 2

Two-Dimensional Speech-Forms

The kind of *mashal* the synoptic writers tell us Jesus habitually used is characterized by the way in which it creates an impact by presenting a logical package which is then referred to the subject matter. It is the presence of this self-authenticating 'logic' that distinguishes such *meshalim* from the allegorical kind, in which utterly unconvincing features in the story are by no means out of place.[1]

I can demonstrate this most succinctly by comparing a parable of Jesus with a saying of the prophet Ezekiel:

> A city set on a hill cannot be hid. (Mt. 5.14)

> A great eagle with great wings and long pinions, rich in plumage of many colours, came to Lebanon and took the top of the cedar; he broke off the topmost of its young twigs and carried it to the land of trade, and set it in a city of merchants... (Ezek. 17.3, 4)

If one forgets for a moment the referents of these *meshalim* and simply compares them as isolated sayings it is at once clear that, though both get their effect by appealing to peoples' experience of the world about them, the first uses this experience to deliver a self-authenticating logic, whereas the second treats the story element most casually with no attempt to make it convincing in its own terms.

It is this distinction in form that dictates the radically different ways in which these two types of sayings are used to refer to their subject matters. Consequently, if one should hear examples spoken in context it would be natural to understand as *illustrative likenesses* those stories which rely on the intrinsic power of their logic; whereas it would be equally natural to comprehend as *allegories* those stories that appear strange and lacking in mundane credibility—but more of this later.

---

1. Cf. Drury, 'Parable', p. 510; on Ezekiel's *meshalim*.

I base my arguments concerning the form of the parable-*mashal* (henceforth referred to simply as parable) on a presupposition generally acceptable to all, except some of those of the school of the new hermeneutic: that such figures of speech are two-dimensional, one dimension being that of the 'story' and the other (using the generally recognised vocabulary) that of the 'application'—the subject to which the 'story' refers.

Take this example I found in the Guardian newspaper of 7 Febuary 1980.

PAKISTANIS—A PEOPLE WITHOUT HOPE
Report from Peter Niesewand in Rawalpindi.

It is a difficult year for the Pakistan government. Russia has moved into Afghanistan, threatening the western frontier, and Pakistan's old enemy, Mrs Ghandi, has romped back to power in India, making the eastern frontier look suddenly insecure. But people in the Pakistan province of Sind were celebrating. A visitor there said: 'There was jubilation. They were handing round sweets and behaving as if twin sons had just been born.' It was one sign of the new, disturbed, nihilistic times. There were many others. In Islamabad, the capital, a man was asked if the threat from Russia meant Pakistanis would now rally round the military ruler, General Zia ul-Haq. He answered with this parable: 'A man was leading a heavily laden donkey along a mountain path when suddenly he saw bandits approaching. The man shouted to his donkey "Run! Run!" The donkey turned to him and said "Whoever is my master I will be just as heavily laden as I am now. You run!"'

In this parable the 'story' is the tale of the master and his donkey and the 'application' the political situation in Pakistan in 1980, to which the questioner was referring when he asked whether Pakistanis would rally round their ruler.

If we take this two-dimensionality as read it immediately becomes possible to set to one side a number of sayings of Jesus that are not to be confused with parables. In this category are Jesus' paradoxical remarks, like the first being last and the last first (Mk 9.35), since these are clearly one-dimensional. And we can discard for now those texts in which Jesus points to someone's model behaviour, for example the story of the widow's mite (Mk 12.41, 42), although I shall be dealing with this point more fully later.

Even having excluded such one-dimensional forms from consideration we still face the problem that parables share a genuine two-dimensional character with a large number of other speech-forms: examples, coded messages, riddles, satires, similes, metaphors, proverbs, to name but a few. To see where parables fit into this general category it helps to recognize that two-dimensional speech-forms fall into three distinct families, each defined by the way in which the two dimensions are interrelated. For convenience I call these the Representation, Instance and Illustration families. As I will show in Chapter 4, parable is a type of Illustration. However, I shall begin by looking at the non-parabolic forms.

The Representation Family

In these forms the user, when speaking about a subject, replaces it with a representation taken from a completely different situation. For example I may speak about a piece of land as being 'Crown property', meaning that it is administered by the government on behalf of the state—the subject being the situation of ownership and administration, and the representation, which I use to replace this rather cumbersome subject, being the Crown.

When I say that in these forms the representation is chosen from a different situation I am indicating that although it may well be taken from real life it has an aspect of unreality in the context in which it is used; as if it had been brought in from another time or place. The essential nature of all representational forms is that although they operate in two dimensions *there is only ever one entity under consideration* for the user automatically relates the representation and the subject so directly that they become identified. It is rather like what happens when you look in the mirror. Here also there are two dimensions, that of the reality and that of the reflection, but only one entity being observed, because though what you look at is simply your image you actually consider it as indistinguishable from yourself. In other words you do not treat your image as if it had a separate existence but talk about looking at yourself in the mirror.

This 'two dimensions—one entity' principle is true of all representations. Thus when talking about Crown property I do not mean to introduce the monarch into the conversation. All I intend is to raise in shorthand the issue of a certain type of ownership and administration. For convenience I call this very direct connection between representation and subject a *one-stands-for-another* relationship.

We should all be perfectly familiar with representations in speech since, properly understood, every word we utter is just another example! When I choose to give my new-born child a name all I am doing is creating a new representation. The strange thing is that though the name I select will, in all probability, be shared by a host of other individuals this does not seem to affect the one-stands-for-another relationship between it and my new offspring. I have several friends called John. However, in any conversation—just so long as I know who is being talked about—that name when it is uttered will for me instantly *be* that person; so much so that it never occurs to me that it is just a representation. Indeed the only time that I am made aware of this fact is when two Johns are being talked about at the same time.

It is this basic one-stands-for-another characteristic that makes of representations excellent tools for dealing with subject matters which, for one reason or another, are difficult to handle since it proves much easier to talk about one's chosen representation than about the subject matter direct. In other words representations are intrinsically facilitators in that they enable people to converse easily about matters that would otherwise be beyond their linguistic capacities.

A second characteristic of representations, as a speech-form, is their relative appropriateness, in that the 'image' they create of the subject, while normally good, is never one hundred percent identical. This fact is often used by the creator of the representation to intrigue the interlocutors so that their attention becomes fixed. I call this phenomenon the 'kick', it being important to realize that this kick is just the useful flow in the representation's general appropriateness.

Take again the mirror analogy. We are all aware that people who have never experienced mirrors find them intriguing. However once they have become used to the mirror's image-producing effect it quickly loses its special appeal and simply becomes a very useful thing to have around the house. However, there are special circumstances in which this appeal can be reawakened. Due to the nature of physical reflections a looking glass reverses its image left to right. This does not bother us usually but there are occasions when it can interfere with our vision. For example though I see my wife every day I rarely have the opportunity of looking at her reflection in the mirror, but when I do I am always struck by the fact that she has a crooked smile. This is odd, because her smile has always been crooked. However, normally I don't notice it and it is only when I see it reversed by the mirror that my brain is alerted to the fact by the switch. It recognizes the image as being of her, of course, for it is virtually exact, but the slight changes brought about by the left to right distortion cause me to take another look.

In the same way people are intrigued by certain representational speech-forms. We call them riddles:

> Little Nancy Etticote
> In a white petticoat
> And a red nose:
> The longer she stands
> The shorter she grows,

What is described here seems to be a girl but is in fact a candle.

The fact that a representation is a mixture of appropriateness and inappropriateness can also be used to confuse listeners so that instead of being fascinated they are upset. In other words the kick can be used to put off rather than to intrigue. Take again the reflection analogy. When you hold up a page of writing to a mirror the left-to-right switch tends to upset you so that you look away. In the same way representational speech-forms can be used to deter people from enquiring further. In cases like this we generally refer to them as encoded messages.

A third characteristic of representations is that they are artificial contrivances. In this respect, of course, they are markedly different from mirror images which, however badly distorted, are always a natural reflection of reality. Because of this it is misleading to talk about representations, as people sometimes do, as if they were ideologically neutral, for the truth is that representations are strongly coloured by the vision of their creators and present the interlocutor with a personal interpretation of reality offered on a take-it-or-leave-it basis. This is why I call representations *assertions*. This characteristic is true, to a degree, of even the simplest figures of speech and the names we give our children. However it tends to be very much more pronounced when it comes to dealing with the sort of extended representations that we find in the Bible—as for example when the prophets speak of Israel as a whore running after her lovers!

> And you, O desolate one, what do you mean that you dress in scarlet, that you deck yourself with ornaments of gold, that you enlarge your eyes with paint? In vain you beautify yourself. Your lovers despise you; they seek your life. (Jer. 4.30)

Let us now look at the individual forms in the representation family.

The Figure

The simplest is the 'figure', which is nothing more than a verbal symbol. In figures one is dealing with a single idea. For example the prophets

handle the complex abstract notion of a free, independent state by referring to it as a 'virgin', thereby making use of the basic one-stands-for-
another characteristic:

> Come down, and sit in the dust, O virgin daughter of Babylon; sit on
> the ground without a throne, O daughter of the Chaldeans! For you shall
> no more be called tender and delicate. (Isa. 47.1; see also Amos 5.2;
> Jer. 46.11; Lam. 1.15)

Similarly Jesus, in common with Rabbinic Judaism, evokes the notion of
the insidious flaw that ends up corrupting the whole person: he speaks
of the 'leaven' of his opponents (Mk 8.15). Likewise he suggests the
way in which the coming time of trouble will purify and refine his disciples' attitude and behaviour, using a double figure in which he describes
how they will be 'salted with fire' (Mk 9.49). On another occasion he
reminds his listeners of the real anguish that this time of trouble will
inevitably bring upon them, employing the prophetic figure of the 'cup'
which brings drunkenness and vomiting and complete loss of self control
(Mk 10.38, drawing on Isa. 19.14; 51.17).

At one point he turns a figure used by his opponents against them.
They glorify the privileged position they hold in life by claiming 'to possess the keys to the Kingdom of Heaven',[2] to which Jesus responds by
saying that all they make of their good fortune is to lock themselves and
everyone else outside! (Mt. 23.13).

He was also capable of turning traditional figures upside down. The
prophets often spoke of the oppressions that people suffered as heavy
yokes, like those which farm animals had to bear (Isa. 58.6). Jesus for his
part made use of this same figure to attract people into discipleship by
claiming that the yoke that *he* wanted to put on them would be a light
one (Mt. 11.29).

The Allegory

The next form in the representation family is the allegory. An allegory is
a complex figure: often one that has been expanded into a veritable
story. As I see it, the distinction between figure and allegory is a matter
of personal judgment since the one naturally blends into the other,
making it a fruitless task to try to delineate the frontier between them.

There are a number of different types of allegory, each defined by
the way in which the characteristics of representations are used: the

2. Jeremias, *Parables*, p. 55.

one-stands-for-another relationship, the appropriateness, and the inappropriateness or kick. As in figures, the one-stands-for-another relationship
makes of allegory a first rate tool for talking simply and straightfor-
wardly about a situation that is naturally cumbersome and hard to
handle. Because modern cultures make use of large political and psychological vocabularies, involving a great many abstract concepts, we can
now discuss very complex social realities without having recourse to
such tools. Indeed, we may unreflectively disparage biblical allegories as
childish and miss seeing them for what they really were: ingenious
devices for putting forward personal interpretations of complex social
realities in simple terms available to everyone.

For example, Ezekiel wished to announce his understanding of the
likely political effect of Zedekiah's breaching of his treaty with
Nebuchadrezzar, king of Babylon. In his place we would have written an
essay full of complex political vocabulary and abstract thought. Lacking
such tools he did the same job by telling a story about two eagles and a
low spreading vine (17.2-10). The difficulty biblical writers experienced
was not confined to handling political subjects for there were spiritual
realities that proved equally difficult to manipulate. Thus we find Ezekiel
speaking about Yahweh's historical dealings with Israel by telling the
story of the rescue of a female child abandoned at birth (16.2-34).

However this facilitating aspect was not the only reason for using allegories. Because of the intriguing characteristic they were sometimes also
used as riddles, designed to fascinate the hearers and fix a message in
the forefront of their minds. Thus the book of Isaiah opens with three
chapters in which the prophet denounces the sins of Judah. He describes
how, having broken the covenant, Judah has brought misery on itself at
God's hand, and proclaims that God will finally bring triumph out of its
downfall. In these pages he delivers condemnation upon condemnation
almost ad nauseam and then suddenly out of the blue introduces his
famous allegory of the vineyard:

> Let me sing for my beloved a love song concerning his vineyard: My
> beloved had a vineyard on a very fertile hill... (5.1)

which ends:

> For the vineyard of the Lord of hosts is the house of Israel, and the men
> of Judah are his pleasant planting: and he looked for justice, but behold
> bloodshed; for righteousness, but behold, a cry! (5.7)

Now it cannot be that Isaiah's intention in introducing this allegory was
simply to bring to his hearers' minds his interpretation of events for he

had surely already achieved this object more than satisfactorily in his first three heavy chapters. No, in this instance the prophet is using the allegory's kick to fix this established interpretation of events in the fore-front of his hearers' minds. In this he is certainly successful for once you have heard the song of the vineyard it is all but impossible to get it out of your mind and, far from leaving you fed to the teeth with the prophet's list of heavy denunciations, the allegory has the effect of settling everything down in its place.

In a number of other cases in the Bible it appears to be the 'off-putting' characteristic that is being used, for such allegories present themselves, superficially at least, as coded messages. Thus it is argued that the author of the Book of Revelation wrote about a vision he had had of the defeat of a beast with seven horns and ten heads in order to communicate to the early Christians, without raising the suspicion of the Romans, his belief that they would soon be vindicated (Rev. 12).

When considering the representations found in the Hebrew Bible a word has to be said about the acted allegories of the prophets Isaiah and Ezekiel:

> In the year that the commander in chief, who was sent by Sargon, the king of Assyria, came to Ashdod and fought against it and took it—at that time the Lord had spoken by Isaiah the son of Amoz, saying, 'Go, and loose the sackcloth from your loins and take off your shoes from your feet,' and he had done so, walking naked and barefoot (Isa. 20.1, 2; see also, e.g., Ezek 12.1-7)

What we have here is the prophets abandoning allegory as a speech-form, because they felt that people were not listening to their interpreta-tion of events, and turning instead to allegory in action. The move was a very effective way of intensifying the power of the message they felt constrained to deliver.

In considering these various types of allegories it is important to rec-ognize that all the basic characteristics of representations are present in all allegories; that the differences in usage described above are only a matter of degree. Thus in Isaiah's song of the vineyard it remains true to say that the simplicity of the allegorical form is used to convey a particu-lar theological (ideological) interpretation of historical events, even though it is perhaps the allegory's kick (the intriguing representation of Israel as a vineyard gone wild) that most strikes the reader. I make this point so as to avoid giving the impression that allegories can be neatly sorted into categories corresponding to the purpose they serve. The fact is that all allegories share the same basic form and therefore to a degree every one of its characteristics.

Furthermore it is most important to be clear about this basic form since the term allegory is used with great imprecision even by scholars of the stature of Dodd and Jeremias. They use it to describe what they consider to be a sort of second-rate approach that they wish to keep at arms length when dealing with parables. However, both are happy to find representations (verbal symbols) in the parables they seek to interpret, so one is left wondering when exactly an allegory is not an allegory.[3]

For my part, I wish to make it quite clear that if *any* element in a story is viewed as a representation then the story *as a whole* has to be treated as an allegory, the reason being that one representation naturally borrows another. Take a story concerning a master and two slaves. You might start by only wanting to identify the master as God. But matters will not rest there for this relationship of itself will cause your hearers to see one servant as representing one sort of human being and the other another sort, till even the relationships between the characters will begin to take on a representational significance. It is not the number or even the quality of symbolic references in a story that counts but the fact that the mind has been put into the representational gear.

The 'two-dimensions—one subject' principle of representations holds as true for allegories as for figures. For example when Hosea talks about taking a prostitute for a wife, of having children by her and giving them strange names, it is obvious that what he is talking about is not so much his personal story as a revelation to the community of the catastrophic end towards which it is heading. So, even though his talk is of his wife and children, everyone knows that his dominating interest is in the fate of the community in view of its behaviour and that this is the subject of his references.

Finally, a word of caution. Since allegories are complex and by nature representational, the tendency is for people to regard their operation as somehow diffuse. Dodd writes:

> The typical parable... presents one single point of comparison. In all allegory, on the other hand, each detail is a separate metaphor, with a significance of its own.[4]

---

3.   For example, see the treatment of the parable of The Rebellious Tenants by Dodd, *Kingdom*, p. 98; and Jeremias, *Parables*, p. 76.

4.   Dodd, *Kingdom*, p. 18.

I see this as a profoundly mistaken view since it is manifestly not the purpose of biblical allegories to make a series of points, however connected, but to put forward a unified understanding of a given subject matter. The characteristic that distinguishes allegory from parable is not the number of points that each of them make but that, whereas parable is basically designed to open the listener's eyes,[5] allegory is concerned simply to put forward a given ideological interpretation on a take-it-or-leave-it basis; to say to the interlocutor 'This is how I believe things stand'. It is for this reason that I describe allegories as *extended assertions*.

Mythical Imagery

One further form of representation commonly found in the Bible is mythical imagery. I have already pointed out that representations are facilitators which make it possible to talk about matters that would otherwise be difficult if not impossible to handle linguistically. This is equally true of myth. The fundamental difference between myth and allegory is that, whereas allegory is constantly inventing fresh representations to stand for the new subject matters people want to discuss, myth involves the creation, once and for all, of an enveloping superstructure within which an infinity of themes can thereafter be played out.[6]

There are other differences too which are a function of this basic distinction. For example it is often the author himself or someone in his cultural tradition who invents the allegorical framework, so naturally he is aware that he is using representations. This is quite untrue of those who use the mythological framework since its history goes back into the mists of time. Even people today are usually unaware that they are using representations when they employ the mythological superstructure, for example when they speak of guardian angels. So the chances are that this was considerably more true of the people of the ancient world, who were less aware, perhaps, of the boundary between myth and reality.

It is interesting to note how rarely Jesus is recorded as using mythical imagery.[7] The only unequivocal instance is when he told a little story

---

5.   See below, p. 71.

6.   The mythological superstructure organizes, in terms of spirits and deities, all the various forces that humans experience within the universe.

7.   See list under *Mythical Imagery*, p. 117 below. The reader will infer from this that I consider Jesus' common usage of God, heavenly father, kingdom and last judgment as well as his few references to the devil and to angels to be something

about the adventures of an unclean spirit (Mt. 12.43, 44). Indeed he is comparatively rarely presented as using representative speech-forms at all and even when he does these are generally idiomatic expressions: part of everyday Jewish vocabulary.[8] This may have been because representations are part of the 'in' language of a particular group since you have to be conversant with the representative references in order to appreciate what is meant.[9] In other words representative language is comparable to the telling of an 'in' joke: you don't really 'get it' until you become part of the group. Apparently Jesus was prepared to employ in a minor way the representative speech-forms of the Jewish community of his day but otherwise found little need for such a mode of communication.

The Instance Family

In instances the subject referred to is a *generality* and the user provides his or her interlocutor with an *instance* of this generality.

The essential character of any family of two-dimensional speech-forms is determined by the relationship that they express between these dimensions; in this case between the generality and the instance. What first strikes one about this relationship is that it is between something which is concrete and something which is a pure abstraction. In other words the generalities that constitute the subjects of these speech-forms are really only ideas that people have created. When looking at the world around them they have noticed that some of the things which they have seen share a common characteristic.

So, people found that individuals sometimes misrepresented what had taken place and sometimes struggled to describe things as they really

different from mythical imagery as I have defined it. These are evocations of what one might call 'the religious question'. I do not intend to try to justify this stance here since it would take a whole new book to do so.

8.   See list of representations p. 117 below. In my view the figurative allegorizations which are read into the parables are not original to Jesus.

9.   Scott recognizes this feature in connection with myth: 'a mythic culture discovers uniqueness in the group, not in individuality... It is the triumph of the group over the individual: it demands an empathic and participatory stance, not objectivity. Myth classifies, orders.' Scott, *Hear Then*, p. 39. He uses this characteristic to highlight the difference between myth and parable. Unfortunately he does not realize that this difference simply reflects the fact that they do not share the same basic form— myth being a representation and parable an illustration (see Chapter 4 below).

had occurred. Hence was conceived the general abstract notions of truth and falsehood. Of course, calling truth an abstract notion is not the same as saying that it does not exist. It is simply to say that it does not exist in the same way as an act of truth-telling. In other words if 'truth' exists it is as an abstraction and not as a concrete event.

I describe this relationship between a dimension of the concrete and a dimension of abstraction by saying that in 'instances' we are dealing with things that are essentially *one-of-a-kind*. This is the first and most important characteristic of instances. The second follows from it: since instances are by nature one-of-a-kind they serve essentially as *clarifications* of the abstract generalities that are their subjects.

When it comes to identifying the individual forms within the instance family I have to admit that I can find only one: the common example. Examples can be either simple or complex but it does not seem to have struck anyone that this makes the slightest difference for complex examples do not have a special name. Looking for examples (understood as a form of instance) in the Bible I realized something very remarkable: that they are almost entirely absent (Deut. 19.4-5 being a rare exception). The reason for this is very simple. Though people in modern cultures find examples most welcome because they are so very concrete and easy to grasp, their use is paradoxically an indication of the presence of abstract thought for if speakers were already expressing themselves concretely it stands to reason that they would hardly find it necessary to clarify what they were saying.

Whereas people in our culture have largely mastered the art of abstract thought so that their speech is regularly punctuated with gen-eralities, often of a highly sophisticated order, biblical people operated almost entirely within the realm of the concrete.

One area in which the people of the ancient Near East would have found abstractions really useful would have been in framing their laws. Take what we, with our facility for making generalizations, have come to call with admirable brevity the *lex talionis*—their law of retaliation. Because they were unused to formulating generalizations they discussed this law concretely under the rubric of 'life for life, eye for eye, tooth for tooth, hand for hand, foot for foot, burn for burn, wound for wound, stripe for stripe' (Exod. 21.23-25. See also abridged form in Mt. 5.38). Legal codes largely consisted of actual cases loosely strung together which, since it was necessary to cover the ground, had to be very numerous, making the codes themselves extremely cumbersome. By contrast, though society is infinitely more complex now than it was then, modern legal codes are based on a few general principles that can be easily mastered.

Having said this, the reverse of the coin is that because we use such a lot of abstract thought, we are constantly obliged to clarify what we are talking about by offering our interlocutors concrete examples—something which the people of the ancient Near East seldom had to do.

It is certainly true that the RSV sometimes uses the word example; as for instance in Jn 13.15:

> For I have given you an example, that you also should do as I have done to you.

But here, as in other places (1 Tim. 4.12; Jas 5.10; 1 Pet. 2.21; Jude 7) the writer is not clarifying a bit of abstract thought but appealing to a real life *model* for people to copy. Bultmann is clearly thinking of such model-type examples when he includes in his discussion of 'similitudes and similar forms' a category which he calls 'exemplary stories'; citing among others The Good Samaritan, The Rich Fool, The Rich Man and Lazarus, and The Pharisee and the Publican, for he notes:

> ...the exemplary stories offer examples = models of right behaviour.[10]

The evangelists certainly see Jesus as using such models. In the following example the model is he himself:

> And he took a child, and put him in the midst of them; and taking him in his arms, he said to them, 'Whoever receives one such child in my name receives me; and whoever receives me, receives not me but him who sent me.' (Mk 9.36,37)

In an associated logion he makes a child the model:

> Truly, I say to you, whoever does not receive the kingdom of God like a child shall not enter it. (Mk 10.15)

In yet a third incident the model is a poor widow:

> And he sat down opposite the treasury, and watched the multitude putting money into the treasury. Many rich people put in large sums. And a poor widow came, and put in two copper coins, which make a penny. And he called his disciples to him, and said to them, 'Truly, I say to you, this poor widow has put in more than all those who are contributing to the treasury. For they all contributed out of their abundance; but she out of her poverty has put in everything she had, her whole living.' (Mk 12.41-44)

10. Bultmann, *History*, p. 178 n. 1.

Properly speaking, model-type examples should have no place in a discussion of two-dimensional forms, there being nothing lying behind them, to which they refer. Bultmann recognises this. Nevertheless he feels obliged to include the 'exemplary story' category in his examination of similitudes because even if the logia he is thinking about have what he terms 'no figurative element at all' (i.e., no second dimension) they seem to him to have 'a striking formal relationship to parables'.[11]

I believe he is quite wrong and this is not simply because exemplary stories are one-dimensional. I can find no exemplary stories in the Gospels and have no difficulty in understanding why. When selecting models for people to follow or eschew, it is the part of common sense to take these from real life because of their natural weight of authenticity. The idea of asking people to model their behaviour on fictitious characters would have struck the evangelists (to say nothing of Jesus) as absurd in the same way that we would find someone who modelled himself or herself on Batman. The fact that thousands of preachers and amateur story-tellers are forever presenting children with such fictional exemplary stories only serves to underline my point. So, despite its general credence, the idea that Jesus told stories like The Samaritan and The Rich Fool as fictional examples of the type of behaviour he desired people to emulate or avoid is quite improbable.[12]

The Illustration Family

In this family of speech-forms the user when dealing with a subject creates a likeness of it. For instance, should I report to you that when the headmaster came into his office the boy's knees were shaking like a jelly, the condition of the boy's knees would be the subject and jelly the likeness. So in illustrations one dimension is that of the subject and the other that of the illustration.

It is the way in which this family of speech-forms connects the two dimensions which determines its essential character. Making the point that the subject and illustration exist in separate dimensions highlights the fact that, though they may well be drawn from the same concrete

11. Bultmann, *History*, pp. 177-78.

12. See B.B. Scott's quite similar conclusion that Luke's 'example story' parables: The Samaritan, The Rich Farmer, The Rich Man and Lazarus, and Two Men in the Temple, are a fabrication as such—Scott, *Hear Then*, pp. 28-29. For a further discussion of this question see Pb. 44, pp. 146-53 below.

world, in the context of the subject the illustration gives the impression of having been dragged in from elsewhere; there being a certain absurdity in connecting jelly with the picture of a boy waiting for the headmaster in his office.

You will remember that exactly the same thing was said in connection with the relationship between a representation and its subject. However, whereas in the case of representations we deduced from this point the 'two dimensions—one entity' principle, with illustrations this is not the case. Indeed illustrations can only work where there is *no identification* (confusion) *between subject and illustration*. For example, if I say a woman looks like her sister this only makes sense so long as the woman and her sister are considered as entirely different persons. Thus the principle for illustrations is 'two dimensions—two entities' and I characterize the relationship between dimensions as *one-like-another*.

It would be hard to overestimate the importance of this basic difference between representations and illustrations. That in the one there is an essential identification of entities whereas in the other there is an essential distinction, means that representations and illustrations are not just different speech-forms but are *incompatible*. But more of this later.

A second characteristic of illustrations which flows from this 'two dimensions—two entities' principle is that they involve an active participation of the interlocutor in making the connection and, therefore, a sense of discovery when the connection is made. This means that people on the receiving end of an illustration don't feel as if they have been taught something at second hand, as in the case of representations, but experience a sense of personal achievement. This comes about because the connection beween the illustration and the subject is a likeness which has to be *grasped*. Another way of putting this is to say that in illustrations the user intentionally leaves a *gap* for his audience to bridge by their own initiative.[13]

It might be supposed that representations also have gaps needing to

13. Followers of the new hermeneutic refer to the same phenomenon when they speak of the hearer's participation and of the parable being open-ended: Funk, *Hermeneutic*, pp. 133, 142; Fuchs, *Studies*, p. 220; Crossan, *In Parables*, p. 15; Scott, *Hear Then*, p. 419. They argue that this open-endedness means that one can never replace the parabolic narrative by its supposed meaning. I agree, but at the same time wish it to be understood that this does not imply there is any ambiguity in the thrust, as the new hermeneutic would seem to suggest; see, for example, Scott's talk about polyvalence, *Hear Then*, p. 420.

be bridged in that, as I have already pointed out, the representation is never exact; a feature which is carefully exaggerated in the case of riddles. This, however, would be to confuse the *gap* with the *kick*. People may talk about riddles as if they were meant to be guessed. But the truth of the matter is that if this were the case they would seldom work. In fact, guessing a riddle is all but irrelevant to one's enjoyment of it, for the only two states that really count are: waiting in anticipation for the solution, as in the case of detective stories; or being in the know, as in the case of the Little Nancy Etticote nursery rhyme which small children adore without ever finding the solution for themselves. In complete contradistinction to riddles, with illustrations the only state that really counts is the moment of disclosure, since if that fails all is lost. Perhaps the only disappointment comparable with that of an illustration that fails to disclose is a detective story which the reader sees through or for which the solution is lost.

The third characteristic of illustrations is shared with representations in that both possess a kick (it being understood that whereas the kick in a representation is constituted by an inappropriateness *in the 'naming'*, with an illustration it is an inappropriateness *in the likeness*). For example, supposing I told you that after the thunderstorm my daughter came into the kitchen looking like a wet rag. The strength of this illustration is not only due to the *aptness* of likening a bedraggled girl to a wet rag but also to the *incongruity* of likening a human being to a rag. It is this inappropriateness in the likeness which spices the comparison with that touch of humour.

Taken together, these special characteristics of illustrations make them an ideal means of opening people's eyes to things of which they are unaware. It could be said of illustrations that they act to shed light on situations and it is for this reason that I categorize them in general as instruments of illumination. It is because illustrations are designed to illuminate that their kick is never used to disguise or hide, as it is with representations.

The Simile

The simplest speech-form in the illustration family is the simile, which is an analogy connected by a middle term: commonly 'as' or 'like', for example in the remark 'He fought like a lion'.

In the Hebrew Bible ordinary similes like this are almost always used within a discourse as *descriptive illuminations*, as I call them, the purpose of which is to draw the readers in (or out) so as to make them feel for what is being discussed. This is much in the same way as a modern novelist will begin a chapter with a description of the physical and psychological scene in which his characters are about to play their parts. So Jeremiah brings to his hearers' attention his feelings about the idol-gods of Israel's neighbour by describing them thus:

> They are like scarecrows in a cucumber field, and they cannot speak; they have to be carried, for they cannot walk. (10.5)

However, occasionally the prophets used the illuminating quality of similes more pointedly to exhort, warn, accuse or denounce. Thus Jeremiah chides God for allowing the wicked to prosper and calls on him to change his ways:

> Pull them out like sheep for the slaughter, and set them apart for the day of slaughter. (12.3)

Likewise Hosea attacks the priests of Gilead, declaring:

> As robbers lie in wait for a man, so the priests are banded together; they murder on the way to Shechem, yea, they commit villainy. (6.9; see also 5.10; 7.6 and Jer. 20.16)

In order to distinguish these similes from the more common descriptive illuminations I call them *emphatic illuminations* since the awareness they call forth is used in a rather strong and assertive manner; though it has to be admitted that the distinction is but a matter of degree and that descriptive and emphatic illuminations are really only the end terms of a continuum.

The fact of the matter is that ordinary similes do not readily lend themselves to emphatic usages, so it is hardly surprising that ways were found to 'crank them up' artificially so as to make them more suitable for the occasion. For example, similes were strengthened by using them in pairs, as in these words that Hosea put into the mouth of God:

> I am like a moth to Ephraim, and like dry rot to the house of Judah. (5.12)

An even better way of making a simile capable of carrying an emphasis was to use it against its natural bent:

> As a well keeps its water fresh, so [Jerusalem] keeps fresh her wickedness... (Jer. 6.7)

This object could be achieved also by means of 'dissimiles'. For example Isaiah denounces Israel in these terms:

> The ox knows its owner and the ass its master's crib; but Israel does not
> know, my people does not understand. (Isa. 1.3; see also Amos 6.12;
> Jer. 2.32; 8.7)

According to the synoptic Gospels, Jesus used both descriptive and
emphatic similes. They also include a couple of his emphatic 'dissimiles'.[14] However, they make it clear that the typical way Jesus strengthened similes was to create a comparison that emphasized the likelihood
of the outcome it was out to prove. For example, when trying to get
people to keep in perspective such mundane matters as guaranteeing for
themselves enough food and clothing Jesus gave this comparison:

> Look at the birds of the air: they neither sow nor reap nor gather into
> barns, and yet your heavenly father feeds them. Are you not of more
> value than they? (Mt. 6.26)

'Of more value', here, adds emphasis which a straight likeness—for
example, 'why should it be different for you?'—does not have.

Two other examples of this particular kind of simile are of especial
note. In the first Jesus turns this 'more-than' form inside out when he
claims that it is easier for a camel to go through the eye of a needle than
for a rich man to enter the kingdom of heaven (Mk 10.25), the basic
analogy being:

> As it is impossible for   So it is more than impossible
> a camel to go through   for a rich man to enter the
> the eye of a needle   kingdom of God.

In the second he reinforces the more-than simile by running it in parallel
with an entirely distinct metaphor, when he warns his disciples that if his
enemies have called the master of the house Beelzebul, how much more
will they malign those of his household (Mt. 10.24), the basic simile
being:

> As they have called me   So how much more will they
> Beelzebul   malign you.

while the analogy behind the added metaphor is:

> As I am to you   So is the master to his servants.

The Metaphor

The second speech-form among the illustrations is the metaphor, which
is created simply by removing the simile's middle-term and compacting

14. See catalogue at end of Part I, p. 118 below.

the two sides of the analogy. Thus 'He fought like a lion' becomes 'He was a lion in the fight'.

The question is what effect this compacting has? You might expect that confusing the subject with its illustration would destroy the gap and transform the speech-form into a 'one-stands-for-another' representation. However, this bringing of the subject and its illustration into the closest proximity actually has the opposite effect. The unnatural juxtaposition of the two entities hits you in the eye, thus heavily underlining the basic appropriateness and inappropriateness—the illustration's kick—while leaving the gap completely untouched, since one is left in no doubt that one is still dealing with a likeness to be discovered rather than an asserted re-naming. It is this exaggeration that gives the metaphor its characteristic punch and makes it naturally more emphatic than the simile.

In the Hebrew Bible metaphors are regularly used to form descriptive illuminations laced with irony. Thus Hosea ridicules Israel for the new international set that has grown up in her midst along with her wealth:

> Ephraim mixes himself with the peoples; Ephraim is a cake not turned.
>
> (7.8)

Mostly, however, the natural vigour of metaphor is employed in producing more emphatic illuminations. Thus Amos denounced the rich women of Samaria, by comparing them with the sleek, fat, idle cattle grazing on the lush pastures east of the sea of Galilee:

> Hear this word, you cows of Bashan, who are in the mountain of Samaria, who oppress the poor, who crush the needy, who say to their husbands, 'Bring, that we may drink!' (4.1)

And Jeremiah had God accuse Judah of breaking faith, in these terms:

> My people have committed two evils: they have forsaken me, the fountain of living waters, and hewn out cisterns for themselves, broken cisterns, that can hold no water. (2.13)

Judging from the synoptic Gospels Jesus' metaphors differed from the prophets' in that they tended to shift towards the sublime or the grotesque. So he calls on his followers to start chopping off their limbs (Mt. 18.8) and go fishing for people (Mk 1.17). Or he describes himself as giving his life as a ransom (Mk 10.45), and his enemies as swallowing camels (Mt. 23.24).

What Jesus is doing here is reinforcing the illumination of his subject at the 'expense' of the illustrative material he is using. Thus in the metaphor of the speck in the brother's eye (Mt. 7.3-5) his talk about a beam makes very good sense in the terms of the subject—it is true that our sins are enormous as compared to the behaviour we criticize in others. It is only in the terms of the illustration that this beam becomes grotesque.

Likewise in the metaphor of straining out the gnat, Jesus' talk about swallowing a camel is perfectly to the point, since there exist self-righteous people (ourselves, from time to time?) who manage not to notice the horrendous acts of lovelessness that fill their lives while taking inordinate care to avoid perfectly trivial sins. It is only the illustration—of a person swallowing a camel—which is fanciful.

This shift towards the grotesque is the result of a decision to increase the effect of one's comparison by basing it on an unlikeness rather than a likeness. By doing so, one is able to use the inherent contradiction either, as is most common, to emphasize the absurdity of something that has taken place or, alternatively, to highlight its curious appositeness—I think for example of the proverbial metaphor in Ezekiel 18.2 that 'the fathers have eaten sour grapes, and the children's teeth are set on edge'.

I have noted that this emphasis is achieved at the illustration's 'expense'. However, I put this in inverted commas so as to let it be understood that I did not mean that the basic analogy was damaged in the process. The gap remains intact since it still remains obvious that one is dealing with a comparison—though now in a negative form.

This brings me to my final point about metaphors which is that they are reinforced or strengthened in a completely different way from similes.

Consider the simile in Mt. 6.26: Jesus does not say:

> You are... like... the birds which God feeds.

He says:

> You are... *of more value than*... the birds which God feeds.

In other words he strengthens his basic simile by increasing the gap between subject and illustration, and he does this by modifying the middle term.

Now, consider the metaphor in Mt. 8.22. Jesus does not say:

> Let those people who involve themselves with death bury their dead.

He says

> Let *the dead* bury their dead.

Here a preoccupation with burying dead relations is used to evoke the way in which people habitually seek to avoid life. Jesus employs this illustration metaphorically, so there is no middle term to manipulate; no gap to widen. Instead he exploits the possibilities offered by compaction and we end up with the macabre, yet telling, image of the dead burying the dead.[15]

The same sort of thing happens in Mt. 6.3. Jesus does not say:

> Give alms with your right hand while your left hand gets on with life.

He exploits the metaphor's compaction, thereby creating this splendidly bizarre illustration:

> Do not let your left hand know what your right hand is doing.

One final example to drive home the point. In Mt. 7.15 Jesus uses the picture of dangerous people as ravenous wolves. However, he does not simply say to his hearers:

> Beware of false prophets for they are ravenous wolves.

He strengthens the metaphor at the illustration's 'expense' by saying:

> Beware of false prophets who come to you in sheeps' clothing but inwardly are ravenous wolves.

15. This entails removing the logion from Matthew's context—the only way in which I can make sense of it. As I see it, Matthew has given it an anachronistic reference to the expected parousia.

Chapter 3

THE EVOLUTIONARY VERSUS THE CLASSICAL APPROACH

Before moving on to deal with the parable and its associated forms I want to draw attention to the advantages of using what might be called an 'evolutionary' approach to two-dimensional speech forms which I mapped out in Chapter 2. When this method is employed each individual trope is seen as developing from formal roots, with the more complex forms succeeding the simpler ones, instead of the more 'classical' approach, adopted for example by J.M. Soskice in her *Metaphor and Religious Language*, in which an attempt is made to distinguish 'higher' from 'lower' forms.

The evolutionary scheme is of course no more than a hypothetical convenience, a useful way of looking at tropes as a whole, since we do not know for certain how language itself developed. This perhaps explains why it has been more usual to consider such speech-forms in terms of how our understanding of them has grown from Aristotle through to the present day, since this is a development that we can be relatively certain about.

However, the fundamental problem with the classical approach is that it leads philosophers or theologians straight into debates in which a quite unnatural characterization of tropes distorts their vision and plays havoc with the definitions. For example, for the seventeenth-century rationalists the debate was: 'pure argument' versus 'ornament' whereas for the new hermeneutics it is: 'creative language' (i.e. language that cannot be conveyed by prosaic or discursive speech) versus 'ornamental language'.[1]

---

1. Hobbes: 'The absurdity of Philosophers that they use 'metaphors, Tropes, and other Rhetoricall figures'; Locke: 'Since wit and fancy find easier entertainment in the world than dry truth and real knowledge, figurative speeches and allusion in language will hardly be admitted as an imperfection or abuse of it'. Cited in J.M. Soskice, *Metaphor and Religious Language* (Oxford: Clarendon Press, 1985), p. 12.

I have already touched on this problem when dealing with a passage in the work of Robert Funk in which he seeks to make a distinction between comparisons that are merely illustrative and those which are creative of meaning.[2] He wants to attribute this *functional* distinction, taken from the above debate, to the *formal* difference between simile and metaphor but is forced to concede that he cannot make it stick.

Crossan tries to avoid the difficulty by attributing this functional distinction to two different types of metaphor: those that simply 'illustrate information' and those that 'create participation'. In the first category he includes allegories, examples and didactic figures and in the second, poetic metaphor—parables and myths.[3]

But this only displaces the problem for readers are still left wondering what it is exactly that produces this functional distinction. Is Crossan trying to draw attention to an unnamed formal differentiation, for example the one I have described between illustrations on the one hand and representations and instances on the other? This might be the case; for it is certainly true that all illustrations, from the simplest simile to the most complex parable, require the hearer to participate by calling on his or her experience in a way not paralleled by representations and instances.[4] However, Crossan's inclusion of myth in his category of poetic metaphor would seem to argue against this supposition since myth (in terms of form) is not an illustration but a representation and although it involves the hearers in an interesting story it does not require them to participate in the sense that I have described above.

Readers are not helped in making a judgment on this matter: first by the fact that Crossan is unclear about the way in which he is using the word 'participation';[5] and secondly because he does not indicate into which of his categories other illustrative speech-forms, like simile and proverb, fall.

Of course it could be that Crossan and Funk are not really interested in matters of form and all they are saying is that two-dimensional speech-forms as a whole can be used either to illustrate information or to

---

2.   See above, p. 17.

3.   Crossan, *In Parables*, p. 15.

4.   Participation seems to be what Funk means by comparisons that are 'creative of meaning': 'It [the metaphor] endeavors to let the next one see what the previous one saw but to see it *in his own way*. As a result, it opens onto a plurality of situations, a diversity of audiences, and the future' (Funk, *Hermeneutic*, pp. 142-43).

5.   Crossan, *In Parables*, pp. 12-19.

create participation and that Jesus' parables (although not necessarily those of the rabbis) should always be seen as doing the latter.

To understand what I am driving at take the simile that two people are like chalk and cheese. I can use this expression to *illustrate information* by telling a friend that I don't know how two individuals manage to get along together and when he asks what I mean, *explaining* that they are like chalk and cheese. On the other hand I can use the same expression to *draw out my friend's participation* when, seeing the same couple walking down the street, I comment without elaboration 'Aren't those two like chalk and cheese'.[6]

The fact is, that Crossan is simply experiencing the difficulty bequeathed to him by Funk of finding some way to impose on the tropes this functional distinction between creative language and mere ornamentation. It is a real curse because it simply cannot be done, for this distinction does not belong with them and has only been dragged in as a result of the misconceived classical debate.

J.M. Soskice goes further then Funk and Crossan in recognising the difficulty. She makes it clear that if you select *striking* similes to compare with metaphors you find that while being textually different they are 'functionally the same', so in such cases the presence or absence of the comparative term 'like' is immaterial.[7] In other words you can only make the functional difference between a 'simple comparison' and a 'richer interactive meaning' coincide with the formal distinction between simile and metaphor if you deliberately choose insipid similes.

However, instead of realizing that this must indicate something wrong with the distinction between 'interactive meaning' and 'simple comparison', Soskice continues the hopeless exercise by doing a Crossan in reverse. Whereas he tried to find the roots of this spurious differentiation within metaphor, she tries to find them within simile. 'A useful distinction can be made in terms of function, between what might be called 'illustrative' similes and 'modelling' similes'.[8]

---

6.   Since this difference is in usage, we are dealing with a matter of degree; one expression playing down the emotiveness of the illustration's thrust and the other enhancing it. However, if usage is all that Crossan and Funk are concerned about here, how does one explain their continual references to specific speech-forms such as simile, metaphor, allegory, example, parable and myth, when talking about this functional differentiation?

7.   Soskice, *Metaphor*, pp. 58-59.

8.   Soskice, *Metaphor*, p. 59.

To elucidate this difference she gives two examples taken from a novel by Henry James:

> A dissatisfied mind, whatever else it may miss, is rarely in want of reasons; they blossom as thick as buttercups in June.

and

> Her mind was to be his—attached to his own like a small garden-plot to a deer park. He would rake the soil gently and water the flowers; he would weed the beds and gather an occasional nose-gay. It would be a pretty piece of property for a proprietor already far reaching.

She comments that while the second of these similes 'provides a model susceptible of considerable development' the first 'is largely illustrative, and serves to emphasize the numerousness of reasons for being dissatisfied'.

But the first example in by no means merely 'illustrative'—meaning by this a decorative way to stress the abundance of the causes of dissatisfaction. Indeed, to use Soskice's own terms this first example offers a perfectly respectable model, stretching far beyond an ornamental raising of the idea of numerousness, since it also includes an awareness of a higgledy piggledy, disorganized spontaneity of growth.

In fact what she presents us with is two 'model'-type illustrations (there being no other type!) the only difference between them being the extent to which each model is amenable to development.[9] So once again the reader is being asked to accept this perverse classical distinction between 'essential' and 'disposable' comparisons without being given the trace of a clear-cut formal differentiation on which to base it.[10]

But the damage due to the classical approach goes further still. It not only interferes with an understanding of the individual speech-forms, obscuring how they are to be distinguished from one another, but it also leads to an unjustifiable denigration or, alternatively, exaltation of the tropes.

For example, it has become almost commonplace to speak dismissively of simile as a purely decorative way of saying things the meaning of which could be put equally well in a straightforward manner. Soskice

---

9.   In these two paragraphs the words 'illustrative' and 'model' are to be understood in Soskice's sense, not mine!

10.   'We have argued that tropes may be distinguished from each other by form, and some more importantly by cognitive function', Soskice, *Metaphor*, p. 62. I feel this is an evasion of the issue.

is aware of this danger. She argues that it is wrong to assume that one speech-form is superior to another since each does a different job, and nothing is served by using a supposedly superior form when a supposedly inferior one is called for.[11]

However, this does not save her from calling synecdoches (e.g. 'the ships opened fire') and metonyms (e.g. 'the White House said yesterday') 'primarily ornamental ways of naming', with all that is implied. This only goes to show how pernicious is the influence of the classical approach, since there is nothing in the least bit ornamental about these speech-forms. In fact they constitute extremely useful shorthand. It is true that they can be replaced by straightforward discourse: 'The sailors on the ships opened fire with their ships' guns' and 'A spokesperson for the President said yesterday'; however, this is a long way from making them ornamental. As with most representations, like the allegories in the Hebrew Bible, they offer ease of handling, not embellishment, so the fact of their being replaceable is supremely irrelevant.

Soskice goes on to assert that '*metaphor goes beyond the role of ornament*' (my italics) as in synecdoche and metonymy.[12] This is equally problematic not only because of its implication that metaphor is superior but also because it shows that all three speech-forms are being treated as compatible. Metaphor is a likeness (illustration) and synecdoche and metonymy are namings (representations). To suggest that one goes beyond the other is therefore meaningless. All that can be said is that they do different things.

The classical approach lets itself down most obviously when the wonders of metaphor and the lesser speech-forms that reflect its glory are described. Thus, for example, Wilder: 'a true metaphor or symbol is more than a sign, it is a bearer of the reality to which it refers'.[13] And Crossan: '…metaphor can also articulate a referent so new or so alien to consciousness that this referent can only be grasped within the metaphor itself'.[14] Soskice is barely more restrained:

> a metaphor is genuinely creative and says something that can be said adequately in no other way, not as an ornament to what we already know but as an embodiment of a new insight.[15]

11. Soskice, *Metaphor*, p. 60.
12. Soskice, *Metaphor*, p. 57.
13. Wilder, *Language*, p. 92
14. Crossan, *In Parables*, p. 13
15. Soskice, *Metaphor*, p. 48

In fact this creative aspect they all speak about in rather extreme terms is not a feature only of select higher tropes—whether metaphor, or metaphor and some similes, or some metaphors and some similes—but of all illustrations without exception. It has a formal basis in the one-like-another character that distinguishes illustrations from one-stands-for-another representations and one-of-a-kind instances. Each and every illustration generates a peculiar combination of thrust and kick, delivering to the listener a particular impact which is experienced as 'creative'.

Since this essential creativity is present in all illustrations everything which Wilder, Crossan and Soskice attribute to it when speaking of metaphor should also apply to a humble simile like 'The cat's eyes were as black as coal'. But it does not, and it is this that demonstrates how inflated their descriptions are. People would rightly laugh if one were to claim that there was 'an intrinsic and inalienable bond' between the experience of a cat's dilated pupils and the coal simile but the fact is that it is just as pretentious to talk about Jesus' parables in such terms.[16]

Let me clarify what I am saying by a little analogy. In our family my father and my brother were noted for their love of parsnips whereas my sister and I were well known as hating them. It was not unusual therefore to hear someone remark at table 'I've found a parsnip!'. Now a philosopher would be the first to point out that the full and precise significance of such a logion can only be properly established by knowing who made it. In other words there is a personal character about the remark 'I've found a parsnip' which contributes to its meaning.

There is a comparable peculiarity attributable to all likenesses, only instead of springing from the personal characteristics of those who voice them this peculiarity is the result of the special features of the comparison itself. So, just as it is true to say that my brother and I did not mean quite the same thing on exclaiming 'I've found a parsnip', so it is true to say that any illustrative likeness is intrinsically unique since no two comparisons make quite the same impact.

However, one should not conclude too much from this fact for just as there was a great deal of similarity in my father's and my brother's personal love of parsnips, making their expressions of joy in finding one in their food extremely similar if not exactly the same, so it is equally true to say that it is usually not too hard to find close counterparts for most likenesses.

16. Crossan, *In Parables*, p. 22.

Take this metaphor that Soskice cites from Virginia Woolf:[17]

> Never did anybody look so sad. Bitter and black, half way down, in the darkness, in the shaft which ran from the sunlight to the depths, perhaps a tear formed; a tear fell; the waters swayed this way and that, received it, and were at rest. Never did anybody look so sad.

Soskice is right to say that there is something unique about this metaphor but unwise to suggest that its meaning can be vouchsafed in no other way.[18] Indeed it reminds me strongly of the psalmist's description of his despair as the experience of sinking in a mire or being drowned in deep waters or being swallowed up by a pit (Ps. 69.14, 15).

The clear conclusion to all this is that we would do better to forget these burdensome and inappropriate classical distinctions and adopt instead an evolutionary approach in which tropes are understood simply in terms of the developmental possibilities provided by their general form and individual features. To clarify, I shall give an example of the classical and evolutionary approaches at work on the same subject matter. Take the phrase 'The pages were covered with a writhing script'. Soskice notes that this is a particularly interesting example of metaphor, due to the absence within it of two clearly contrasted entities: there being no opposite number for 'script'.[19] Since she has adopted the classical approach with its tendency to polarize high and low forms—creative tropes and replaceable embellishments—it is necessary to take account of this kind of oddity when writing up her general definition of metaphor, because such a definition must embrace all that is interesting about this highest of forms.[20]

The result is that when she finally produces her definition its terms are, of necessity, so general as to make it useless as a means of distinguishing metaphor from other tropes. Indeed you could easily use it as a definition of two-dimensional speech-forms as a whole: 'Metaphor is that figure of speech whereby we speak about one thing in terms which are seen to be suggestive of another.'[21]

---

17. Soskice, *Metaphor*, p. 47.

18. 'What is identified and described is identified and described uniquely by this metaphor', Soskice, *Metaphor*, p. 48.

19. Soskice, *Metaphor*, p. 20.

20. 'The Comparison theory has been criticized on the grounds that, while making the metaphorical attribution intelligible, it fails to explain what is interesting about it', Soskice, *Metaphor*, p. 26.

21. Soskice, *Metaphor*, p. 15.

If you adopt the evolutionary approach there is no bother about constantly having to make adjustments in your definitions to take account of every new twist in the development of the speech-form. You take it for granted your definitions are points of departure which differentiate the speech-form you are dealing with from what has 'come before', in a hypothetical sense. Thus a definition of simile as *a verbal likeness drawn between two subjects* and of metaphor as *a compacted verbal likeness* is quite sufficient since the first clearly distinguishes similes from representations and instances, while the second clearly distinguishes metaphor from simile.

In other words, taking the evolutionary approach one's interest lies not at the point of definition but in understanding how the possibilities of a particular trope have been developed. So, to take the 'writhing script' metaphor: The hypothetical likeness on which this is built looks something like this, 'The pages were covered in a scrawling script like some writhing worm'. This is then compacted: 'The pages were covered in a scrawling script, a writhing worm.'

One of the interesting possibilities provided by compaction is that of taking for granted certain elements of the comparison and thus allowing them to drop.[22] In this case the adjective 'scrawling' in the subject-dimension and the noun 'worm' in the illustration-dimension disappear and one terminates with the likeness in its most elegantly abbreviated form: 'The pages were covered in a writhing script.'

I am not for a moment suggesting that anything like this occurs in the mind of the writer. It is just that such a possibility of allusive abbreviation has arisen in our culture and individual writers take advantage of it.

All this is passed over unnoticed by Soskice in her anxiety to produce a worthy definition. However, it is not so much a worthy definition that is important as an understanding of the mechanics (form and function) of the tropes and it is this aspect that is put to the fore in the evolutionary approach.

---

22. This is a typical feature in compacted parables. See Pb. 64, p. 141 in Part II below.

Chapter 4

PARABLES AND RELATED SPEECH-FORMS

Parables

It is clear, even from a superficial examination, that parables are built on likenesses and therefore belong within the illustration family. So just as, in Chapter 2, we set aside the idea that they were models or examples, we can now dismiss any notion of them as figures, allegories, riddles, coded messages or any other form of representation.

Dodd wrote what many scholars[1] consider to be a classic definition of the parable.

> At its simplest the parable is a metaphor or simile drawn from nature or common life, arresting the hearer by its vividness or strangeness, and leaving the mind in sufficient doubt about its precise application to tease it into active thought.[2]

If he was right to think that some of Jesus' parables were metaphors rather than similes we should expect to find in them unmistakable traces of compaction. However, none of the parables he examined display any such signs. Indeed, even in my list, which includes many more sayings, only four (The Narrow Door, Treasure from the Storehouse, The Ploughman Who Looks Back and The Kindled Fire) demonstrate compaction.[3]

I make a clear distinction between simile and metaphor, which perhaps Dodd never made.[4] But the suspicion remains in my mind that he made the mistake of believing that Jesus' parables were often metaphors because, at least in Mark's Gospel, many of them appear as illustrations

---

1. R.W. Funk *et al.* (eds.), *The Parables of Jesus, Red Letter Edition: The Jesus Seminar* (Sonoma, CA: Polebridge Press, 1988). See p. 16.
2. Dodd, *Kingdom*, p. 16.
3. Pbs. 64-67 in catalogue at end of Part I, p. 120 below.
4. See above, pp. 44-47.

without subjects. This gives the impression that Jesus was referring to a subject while actually talking about its illustration, thus identifying the two and creating a metaphor. However, though it is noteworthy that a number of parables in the synoptic tradition appear to have 'lost' their subjects this is not a typical characteristic of metaphor. The only sure way of isolating a metaphor is to identify a comparison that contains elements of subject and illustration mixed together. As it is most unusual to find such a mix in parables it will be better to drop, for the moment, the idea of parables as metaphors.[5]

So by a process of elimination, the notion remains that parable is a development of the simile. What then are the characteristics of this form and how can these help to accommodate it within the overall simile frame? In the definition above Dodd claims that parables leave the hearer in doubt so as to tease the mind into thought. But this is the description of a riddle, which is no illustration but a form of representation. Perhaps Dodd would have agreed with the idea of parables as riddles, for apart from the words 'simile' and 'metaphor' there is nothing in his description which would lead one to suppose that he was thinking of them as illustrations. Indeed his sentence can be rewritten, substituting riddle for parable, and representation for simile/metaphor, and still make perfect sense. Of course Jesus' parables *as they stand in the Gospels* are often enigmatic; this being the general point of departure for us all.[6] But that is the problem that the New Testament poses, not the beginnings of its solution. You have only to take a look at parables outside the

---

5.   Funk argues that parables are metaphor (Funk, *Hermeneutic*, pp. 146-47), his object being to make them square with the 'creative art' thesis. For him, simile indicates a mere referential illustration whereas metaphor is something altogether more poetic. (See also Wilder, *Language*, p. 80). He bases his argument on Jeremias's contention that the introductory phrase used in many of the parables— 'The Kingdom of God is like'—is misleading and should be rendered 'It is the case with the Kingdom as with' (Jeremias, *Parables*, pp. 101-102). Funk claims this formula does not mean the kingdom is like one of the elements of the comparison but that 'the parable has some, as yet unspecified, bearing on the subject in hand'. He is right when he goes on to say that 'the parable *as a whole* is to be brought into relation with the subject' rather than one element within it. However, he is unconvincing when he says 'these considerations support the view that parables are metaphorical and should not be taken as similes', since this formal distinction between simple and complex comparisons has nothing to do with the difference between metaphor and simile; both the latter can be either simple or complex.

6.   See p. 10 above.

Gospels, as for example the story of the donkey[7] or the following offering of Rabbi Joshua ben Korhah, to see that, far from intending to obscure, the purpose is to illuminate a subject so that the hearer may be in *no doubt at all* as to its nature:

> How is it with the vine? At first it is trodden under foot and then it is served up on the table of the kings; even so is it with Israel; they are despised in this world, but will be highly prized in the world to come.[8]

So, if the New Testament parables are enigmatic it stands to reason that this is far more likely to be because something untoward has happened to them in the process of their transmission than that it was their nature from the beginning. After all, who ever heard of a simile or metaphor that was intended to hide what it was illuminating? It is amazing that such a curious idea has endured.

I can illustrate the point by referring to the best known parable in the Hebrew Bible. David has devastatingly abused his position as King, with all that that implied, by acting like any despot. He has seduced Bathsheba and then, when she has become pregnant, arranged to have her husband Uriah killed in battle so that he may cover things up by taking her into his harem:

> And the Lord sent Nathan to David. He came to him, and said to him, 'There were two men in a certain city, the one rich the other poor. The rich man had very many flocks and herds; but the poor man had nothing but one little ewe lamb, which he had bought. And he brought it up, and it grew up with him and with his children; it used to eat of his morsel, and drink from his cup, and lie in his bosom, and it was like a daughter to him. Now there came a traveller to the rich man, and he was unwilling to take one of his own flock or herd to prepare for the wayfarer who had come to him, but he took the poor man's lamb, and prepared it for the man who had come to him.' Then David's anger was greatly kindled against the man; and he said to Nathan, 'As the Lord lives, the man who has done this deserves to die; and he shall restore the lamb fourfold, because he did this thing, and because he had no pity.' Nathan said to David, 'You are the man'. (2 Sam. 12.1-7)

Now, was Nathan arresting David with his story's vividness and strangeness, leaving the king in sufficient doubt about its precise application so as to tease his mind into active thought? Of course not! The

---

7.   Page 29 above.

8.   A.F. Feldman, *The Parables and Similes of the Rabbis* (Cambridge: Cambridge University Press, 1924), p. 139.

idea is absurd. What he was doing was 'nailing' David; allowing him no opportunity to worm his way out of his predicament: going public, and so leaving no one at court in any doubt as to the king's guilt.

If Dodd's definition is altogether mistaken, as I think, what instead are the real characteristics of parables? Well, the most obvious, as regards form, is the fact that they are *complex illustrations*: indeed, in many cases full-blown stories. Bultmann tried to settle the parable form by appealing to this fact. Following on the lines laid down by Julicher he drew a distinction between a saying like The Leaven (Mt. 13.33) which he defined as 'a similitude that brings together two facts' and one like The Sower (Mk 4.2-9) which he described as a true parable in that it 'transposes the facts which serve for a similitude into a story'. He further clarified this distinction by saying that a similitude makes a comparison with a 'typical condition or typical, recurrent event', whereas a parable makes a comparison with 'some interesting particular situation'.[9]

Jeremias, for his part, believed that such a distinction was invalid since it arose from an unjustified attempt to force Jesus' parables 'into the categories of Greek rhetoric'. My reason for rejecting it as a formal distinction, however, is rather more basic. The fact is that it is simply not possible to draw a hard and fast line between what is and what is not a story, or for that matter to explain convincingly why a woman baking bread is a typical recurrent event whereas a man sowing a field is an interesting particular situation!

In fact it is fruitless to try to make a formal distinction between one-line parables, like The Town on a Hill (Pb. 32) and more developed kinds. When used in connection with parables the word 'story' has to be understood broadly as the general ensemble that carries the proposed comparison, which means that even 'Which of you' parables, like the Master and his Servant (Pb. 56), can be said to incorporate 'stories'.

That said, there is a characteristic of the parable story that is attributable to its form. *A parable proposes a logical connection of the type: 'if such-and-such a situation pertains then so-and-so follows'.*

There are a number of things to be noted about this critical feature. First, the overall likeness drawn is not to a single entity (as in simple similes) nor even to a relationship (as in most complex similes) but to a logical package of the above type. Secondly, this 'logic' is not narrowly rational but existential. Thirdly, it is the way in which this 'logic' appeals to experience that renders it self-authenticating. Fourthly,

9. Bultmann, *History*, p. 174.

this 'logic' is not 'highfaluting' but at everyone's level.

Further points can be made about the general way in which parables function. For example they are always given in relation to specific problems which they are meant to dispel by the illumination they shed.

Of course such problems present themselves in different ways. In the case of Nathan's parable the trouble was clearly an attitude-defect in David. However, it could equally be a blindness to the consequences of a decision taken. For example, the book of Judges describes how Jotham tried to get the people of Shechem to realise how foolish they had been in electing the scoundrel Abimelech as their king, by telling them the following story. (Regrettably, the proper conclusion of the parable, shown in brackets, does not appear in the text but has to be taken for granted from the sheer logic of the story.)

> The trees once went forth to anoint a king over them; and they said to the olive tree, 'Reign over us.' But the olive tree said to them 'Shall I leave my fatness, by which the gods and men are honoured, and go to sway over the trees?' And the trees said to the fig tree, 'Come you and reign over us.' But the fig tree said to them, 'Shall I leave my sweetness and my good fruit, and go sway over the trees?' And the trees said to the vine, 'Come you, and reign over us.' But the vine said to them, 'Shall I leave my wine which cheers the gods and men, and go to sway over the trees?' Then all the trees said to the bramble, 'Come you, and reign over us.' (And of course the bramble leapt at the invitation because, unlike the others he was a worthless fellow who possessed nothing of any value). (Judg. 9.8-12)

Alternatively the problem which a parable addressed could be something more bookish: the sort of apparent contradiction that any reader of the Hebrew Bible comes across from time to time when studying the texts. Thus we find the rabbis using parables to clear away such problems for their students.

Take Psalm 11.5, 'The Lord trieth the righteous.' Naturally people would be intrigued as to why the Lord should make things difficult for his righteous servants. It would be quite understandable, if untrue, to say that he made things difficult for the wicked but on the surface the declaration that he 'trieth the righteous' is somewhat puzzling. Rabbi Jose Hanina tried to smooth the way for his students, who were struggling with this problem, by telling them this parable:

> When the flax worker knows that his flax is good, he keeps on beating it, and it grows better; he continues to flog it and it improves (it acquires body). But when he knows that the flax is bad he scarcely beats it at all,

and then it bursts. Even so does the Holy One, blessed be He, not try the
wicked, but only the righteous.[10]

Another characteristic of the way in which parables function is that
whereas ordinary similes and metaphors are included in the natural flow
of a conversation parables arrive as an interruption, breaking the flow.
This is achieved by working on the illustration's gap. Nathan did it by
making David think that he was bringing a case to be judged. When the
king fell for this ploy he sprung the trap with the announcement 'You
are the man!'

Of course, Nathan's parable is an extreme example. More usually it is
enough that the 'reply' to the problem is presented unexpectedly in
story form. Thus in the case of the man and his donkey someone asks a
question about the changing loyalty of the people of Pakistan, and the
parable maker somewhat obliquely begins to tell his story. In doing so a
likeness is implied without actually being stated. For the parable-maker
this is a real bonus for it makes it possible to introduce far more complicated comparisons without overburdening the communication.

Because increasing the gap forces the interlocutor to settle his mind
on the chosen issue to the exclusion of everything else, I describe parable as a *concentrated illumination*: my idea being that it acts like a
searchlight to dispel the darkness surrounding a subject. However, I
have to admit a problem about this description: it does not take into
account the fact that it is the interlocutor who actually has to make the
connection. In other words, calling parables concentrated illuminations
may inadvertently give the impression that they involve a one-way process. This would be quite false, for although good parables leave no
room for doubt and bring about awareness in the interlocutors whether
they want it or not, the fact of the matter is that from their point of view
the impression remains that they have arrived at the conclusion by
themselves: *they* make the connection and *they* see. This is the characteristic which exponents of the new hermeneutic refer to when they
describe parables as open-ended.[11]

Perhaps I can home in on this feature in another way by pointing out
that you can never sum up a parable by simply writing out its basic
analogy because, even if you are satisfied that you have managed not to
betray the parable's logic, you remain miles away from describing the

10. Feldman, *Rabbis*, pp. 61-62.
11. See Funk, *Hermeneutic*, p. 142.

full impact on the listener when he or she bridges the parable's gap and makes the connection. You always find that you want to throw such analogies away, for the parable accomplishes something no analogy can—an instinctive assent in the listener, an unavoidable awareness which is nevertheless his or her own discovery.[12]

So, now, I shall attempt to describe the full parabolic mechanism at work. The parable-maker starts by noticing some mental blindness within his interlocutor and then goes on to identify the underlying problem. Were he in the habit of dealing in abstract generalities he would say to himself 'this person appears to be blind to a certain *common awareness*'. However, in biblical times people envisaged matters more concretely and so would have had in mind a collection of *experiences* rather than an abstract awareness, which is why I use the words 'awareness' and 'experience' interchangeably.

What the parable-maker then does is to draw up a simile, from some completely different field of experience, which highlights this particular common awareness. He then presents this new situation to his interlocutors in the form of a 'story' whose logic drives home the nature of this common awareness. At the same time he amplifies in any way he can the element of surprise and interruption so as to catch his hearers off balance and make them wait in concentration on the thrust of the story.[13] This requires consummate skill since his every word must lead

12. It is the followers of the new hermeneutic who are most associated with the idea that you must never substitute a meaning for the parable story and that you must hang on to the latter at all costs. However in espousing this just cause most of them go overboard: arguing that in Jesus' parables there exists a sort of mystical connection between meaning and illustration, making it impossible to have the one without the other. Fuchs, *Studies*, p. 220; Wilder, *Language*, p. 14; Crossan, *In Parables*, pp. 11-13. I find this altogether far-fetched. Once again only Scott, of their number, correctly understands the situation, although he too spoils things by continuing to measure the parable in terms of its meaning: 'The parable does not seek closure... For precisely this reason the parabolic narrative is always primary and can never be replaced by its supposed meaning. The parable is "laid beside", is "like", and therefore its meaning is found in its being laid beside.' Scott, *Hear Then*, p. 419.

13. I am convinced that when Julicher spoke about a parable making a *point* he was seeking to draw attention to the phenomenon of the *thrust*. However, he chose to argue (against the evidence) that whereas a parable possesses one point of comparison an allegory has many. In this way, people's attention became wrongly riveted on the numbers question in relation to the difference between parable and allegory. See, for example, Via's account of the one-point approach to parables (*Parables*, pp. 2-4). This is a pity because, although it goes without saying (in spite of Via's

his listeners inexorably towards the final revelation without sidetracking them or giving things away prematurely. The simile must be perfectly complete yet no room exists for superfluous decoration or embellishment. In the final performance he cannot afford a word too many nor a word too few!

But matters do not end here. The launching of the parable is only half the exercise, the other half being the way it is received. The hearers already have their own, if erroneous, understanding of the subject under discussion. The effect of the comparison, coming as it does as a story—a long-drawn-out interruption and surprise—is to cause them to lower their guard. They pursue the story's logic (to find the *thrust*), make the connection with their own situation (by leaping the *gap*), and then receive the parabolic package in the midst of the circumstances of the moment (as the *impact*). Their eyes are open and despite themselves they see things in a new light.

The reception of the story is very different in the case of an allegory. Here there is no long-drawn-out interruption since the hearers make the translation as they go along. The surprise too is continuous since it stems from a 'carefree' approach—there being no controlling 'logic'. Consequently the story often contains numerous inventive expansions.

I have been very careful in choosing my words when describing how parables work. Normally people talk about the *point* of a parable-story rather than its *thrust*, and about the overall *meaning* of a parable instead of its *impact*. However, this gives the false impression that communicating in parables is an intellectual exercise associated with books, learning and preaching.[14]

I am inclined to think that parables developed out of the cut and thrust of ideological exchange in the market place.[15] The strong

protestations to the contrary) that parables only have one thrust, allegories have none since being representational they can only make assertions; lacking a transferable logic they have no way of putting forward a discoverable comparison.

14. Jungel was the first to spot the error of thinking of parables as rational arguments (see above, pp. 15-16). This correction was taken up by those who followed in the new hermeneutic. For example Funk emphasized the existential and imaginative nature of parables, (*Hermeneutic*, p. 143.) However, they persisted in talking about the *meaning* of parables and so in some ways continued the error (Wilder, *Language*, p. 82; Funk, *Hermeneutic*, p. 150; Via, *Parables*, p. 10).

15. 'Here we have in Jesus' sayings the counterpart of his own person and presence among men: not as a philosopher, priest or scribe but as an artisan, not in the

emotional content in Jesus' stories marks them out as essentially ideological in character. Implicit in them is an insistent questioning as to the kind of world his opponents desire and want to help establish.[16] This explains why they function not as discussion-openers but as conversation-stoppers.[17] Instead of engaging opponents in dialogue in order to lead them to a reasoned point of view, Jesus, through his parables, throws such a light on what his adversaries are about that they are forced to see their attitudes as essentially foolish: as constraining them to operate against their own best interests.

Indeed, in its non-argumentativeness, in its immediacy and carelessness of the future, the parable as used by Jesus has much in common with the political cartoon.[18] This is true despite their dissimilarity, due in large measure to the unashamed negative aspects of the latter—its lovelessness and unconcern with healing.

Now, having understood the way in which the parable mechanism works, I am encouraged to attempt a definition to replace the one by Dodd: *A parable is, by form, a similitude in which the element used for comparison is a self-authenticating 'logic' and, by function, a concentrated illumination. Like all illustrations parables are designed to stimulate awareness.*[19]

Looking at this definition I have to admit that it, too, is beset with difficulties, for all three constitutive features—acting as a similitude, concentrating attention and bringing awareness—are undermined in certain examples. Thus, while I persist in maintaining that parables are similitudes, it would be foolish to deny that even outside of the special literary environment of the Gospels, where I believe the allegorizations are editorial, there exist parabolic 'comparisons' with allegorical features, even if they are comparatively rare:

desert or in the temple but in the marketplace.' Wilder, *Language*, p. 85. By 'marketplace' I do not mean necessarily 'in the public domain' but rather that parables arise spontaneously in the cut and thrust of everyday exchanges rather than in studied teaching relationships.

16. See Dodd, *Kingdom*, pp. 22-23; Bultmann, *History*, p. 198; Funk, *Hermeneutic*, p. 133, on parables as 'inducing judgment'.

17. '[T]hey (the parables) are prophetic in character rather than discursive or argumentative', Wilder, *Language*, p. 92.

18. '[Jesus' speech] is not studied; it is extempore and directed to the occasion, it is not calculated to serve some future hour', Wilder, *Language*, pp. 20-21.

19. Stimulating people to awareness is not the same thing as Dodd's 'teasing their minds into active thought'.

This might be compared unto a king who had a vineyard which three
enemies attacked together. The first began plucking among the small
single branches, the second continued the work of havoc by thinning the
clusters. The third tried to uproot the vines. Even so did Pharaoh order:
'Every son that is born ye shall cast into the river' (Exod. 1.22).
Nebuchadnezzar then tried to diminish the scholars: 'The craftsmen and
the smiths were departed from Jerusalem' (Jer. 29.2); while Haman
sought to uproot the whole vineyard, as it is written: 'To destroy, to slay,
to cause to perish all the Jews' (Esther 3.13).[20]

Likewise it would be wrong to pretend that all parables stimulate awareness since if you dig about amongst those from the rabbis you find some
examples that look as if they stem more from a wish to put on a virtu-
oso performance than a desire to overcome difficulties in the text. As
Rabbi Feldman says

It is true that at times [their] figures of comparison... are in many respects
rather strained; this is due in a large measure to the strong exegetical bent
of the Rabbis, to their innate tendency to exhaust the possibilities of
interpretation:[21]

One cannot evade paying the custom dues on nuts, because by their rat-
tling they make themselves heard and are thus disclosed. Even so it is
with the Israelites: wheresoever one of them may go he cannot say 'I am
not a Jew,' for he is duly recognised, even as it is written: 'All that see
them shall acknowledge them, that they are the seed which the Lord hath
blessed'.[22]

Similarly, though I am perfectly convinced in my own mind that
parable-makers invariably attempt to magnify the gap: to break the flow
of an argument and concentrate attention on the subject matter by the
way they tell their stories, for example by means of a pregnant pause or
a sideways glance, it later becomes all but impossible to prove they have
done so.

How can one deal with such lacunae and discrepancies and so have a
convincing overall picture of the parabolic mechanism? As I see it the
only way in which this can be achieved is by keeping in mind a putative
historical view of the subject.

In the first place we have to imagine individuals in early cultures
realising they were aware of realities that others were blind to and so

20. Feldman, *Rabbis*, pp. 131-32.
21. Feldman, *Rabbis*, p. 15.
22. Feldman, *Rabbis*, p. 179.

starting to search for ways to open people's eyes. Initially it would have been discovered that it often helped people to overcome such problems if they could be given simple comparisons with phenomena of which they were already well aware.[23] A more complex comparison—the parable—was then developed within a specific culture as a well understood speech-mechanism. Then of course, people being what they are, someone came along whose interests were scholarly rather than marketplace orientated who adapted this established speech-mechanism to his own needs. So a few examples arise, such as some among the rabbinical parables, in which the fundamental rules are broken. It is questionable whether such exceptions to the rules are ever successful. In any case, they are but exceptions.

The question now arises whether there is more than one type of parable. If there is, the difference can only be in terms of the sort of problems they address. The simplest parables aim to bring awareness to people who find themselves in a new situation and either make a mistake or in some other way show that they misjudge what is going on. I call these *learner* parables. This is the kind of parable supposedly told by Jotham and the kind habitually used by the rabbis when helping their students with exegetical difficulties. It is also the type of parable that Jesus told the Syro-Phoenician woman and was delighted to discover that she did not need it.[24]

A second type of parable is concerned with perplexing situations in which the parable-maker finds people uncertain about which way to turn because of the conflicting signals they are receiving; for example, the predicament of the disciples when Jesus condemned the Temple and forecast its destruction. The disciples had always been made to believe that the Temple was the heart of Judaism and the last bastion against the outside world's ideological impurity, yet here was Jesus talking as if in God's plans for humanity it was somehow dispensable. How could this be? Jesus illuminated their way through this difficulty by telling them the parable of The Barren Fig Tree, which I call a *dilemma* parable.[25]

A third type of parable is addressed to peoples' attitudes, like the one that Nathan told David to the king's discomfiture. I call these *attitude-straightening* parables. They demonstrate a number of peculiar features:

---

23. 'The stories are so told as to compel men to see things as they are, by analogy indeed', Wilder, *Language*, p. 83.

24. Pb. 11, as listed p. 119 below.

25. Pb. 47, as listed p. 120 below.

First, people with an attitude-defect characteristically operate as if they were unaware that their attitude constitutes a problem; which means of course that they will make no effort to overcome their defect. Consequently the people living with them are obliged to choose either to let them continue to wreak havoc around themselves or else to face up to them, perhaps by using a parable. So, unlike other types of parable, attitude-straightening ones are essentially *confrontational*.[26]

Secondly, when people with an attitude-defect realize that the hunt is on they will instinctively try to get themselves 'off the hook'. It follows that attitude-straightening parables are designed to *corner* the 'prey', leaving no room for escape by a blurring of the issue.

Thirdly, exposing people's defective attitudes causes them great pain. Consequently attitude-straightening parables always risk engendering *conflict* since the chances are that the 'target' will respond not by repenting but by lashing out.[27]

It is extremely unusual to find the rabbis using this type of parable. However the following may be an exception for, though it claims to be just a straightforward elucidation of Ps. 46.9, it clearly addresses what we today would call a racist attitude:

> A stag brought up in the wilderness came of his own free will and mixed with the flock. The shepherd gave him to eat and to drink and bestowed upon him greater affection than on his sheep. Whereupon people said to him, 'Wilt thou tend this stag more affectionately than thy sheep?' And he replied, 'How wearily have I toiled in rearing my flock, leading them out in the morning and bringing them in at nightfall! But this stag, although brought up in the wilderness and forests, joined my sheep of his own free will—shall I not show him special affection?'[28]

Now it is my contention that the great majority of Jesus' parables were attitude-straightening. My reason for adopting this view (and like all

---

26. In understanding Jesus' parables as 'creative art' the new hermeneutic sees no necessity to conceive them in such confrontational terms. For example Funk argues that it is perfectly possible that while some of the parables were directed to hostile critics others could equally have been aimed at people who were friendly to Jesus. (Funk, *Hermeneutic*, pp. 144-45.) In one way I think he was right since Jesus apparently addressed his own disciples with parables. However, this is no argument against the confrontational thesis, which I hold to be right, because a person can confront a friend as well as an enemy to offer healing.

27. On parables as weapons of controversy see Jeremias, *Parables*, p. 21.

28. Feldman, *Rabbis*, p. 226.

other explanations it is just a hypothesis since the specific problems Jesus addressed with his parables were seldom if ever recorded) is threefold:

1. Jesus' ministry would hardly have offered sufficient numbers of occasions of people facing radically new historical or personal crises or dilemmas, apart from his own coming,[29] to explain the sheer quantity of parables we are dealing with in his case.[30] Even the rabbis who used parables as a tool for

---

29. Within the new hermeneutic it has been customary to associate the parables with central themes. Thus Fuchs associates them with Jesus' self understanding, Weder with an anticipation of the resurrection and Scott with the kingdom. Similarly Crossan has grouped a number of stories under the heading 'Parables of Advent' and it could be supposed that these result from Jesus' concern to help people adjust to the radically new situation brought about by his coming. However, even if it is feasible to account for some of the parables in this way the selection process is pretty arbitrary and there will always remain a large number still unaccounted for.

30. I treat all the parables attributed to Jesus by the synoptic tradition and the Gospel of Thomas as original. It is of course impossible to be certain of the genuineness of any of them. Many scholars (e.g. The Jesus Seminar) attempt to assess their historical authenticity by applying Bultmann's basic principle that the more a logion displays the particular stamp of Jesus—a 'characteristic of a new and individual piety' or an 'eschatalogical consciousness'—the more confidence we can have that it comes from him, whereas the more it reflects 'a popular wisdom and piety' and the influence of rabbinic or Jewish apocalyptic thought the less certain we can be that it does (Bultmann, *History*, pp. 104-105). However, such a test is only viable where there is certainty about a logion's subject. Unfortunately, in the case of Jesus' parables we are even less certain about their subject matter than we are about their author! For example, in Pb. 29 does the burglar illustrate in some way an anticipated eschatological crisis? Some scholars suggest it does but they are only guessing. Furthermore the Bultmann test, which is an examination of content, can determine the authenticity only of theological pronouncements. If I am right that parables are healings rather than teachings, Bultmann's principle is as useless in verifying the genuineness of a synoptic parable as of a synoptic miracle. Healings cannot be judged by their content but only by whether they work (See Mk 3.22-26). In other words, there is nothing about the content of a parable story which can be taken as a hallmark of its author. In parables, as with miracles, the stamp of Jesus consists solely in the fact that to the eye of faith what he said or did proved to be of the kingdom, that is, the appropriate way to offer restoration and abundance of life in the circumstances and this is a matter of discernment, one might say of 'recognition'. As far as I can see the only appropriate test applicable to Jesus' stories is the communicative skill shown in their construction since it is clear people considered him a master of the art. However, all the parables in the synoptic traditon and the Gospel of Thomas develop first rate thrusts; which means that there is no possible way of distinguishing between them.

interpreting scripture, thereby providing themselves with unlimited scope, each produced at best a mere handful.

2. It is unlikely that opponents would have reacted as negatively as they did to a person who created learner parables or dilemma parables; whereas it is perfectly understandable that they would have wanted to dispose of someone who used attitude-straightening parables to expose their carefully hidden and most sensitive weaknesses.[31]

3. The evangelists associate Jesus' parables with Isaiah's hardening thesis, which likewise concerns a message that *confronts, corners and risks conflict*. Indeed Isaiah 6.9-10 can be taken as an excellent summary of the task allotted to the attitude-straightening parable-maker.[32]

So although people, like Bultmann, may suspect that the tradition has attributed to Jesus stories taken from elsewhere, the truth is they have nothing firm to go on.

31. See Chapter 5, pp. 103-104 below, for discussion of Jesus' parables as causes of hostility.

32. This text, which describes God as purposely (*hina*) driving his enemies into their contradictions and preventing (*mēpote*) them from repenting, has caused endless difficulties. Because it seems to attribute an unacceptable vindictiveness to God, commentators have attempted to find ways around it. T.W. Manson, in *The Teachings of Jesus* (Cambridge: Cambridge University Press, 1939), argued that *hina* should be read as introducing a result rather than a purpose (pp. 76-80), while Jeremias suggested that it should be taken as indicating the fulfilment of a prophecy. Jeremias also argued that, following the Rabbis, *mēpote* should be read as 'unless' rather then 'lest' (*Parables*, p. 17). The problem with such circumventions of the difficulties is the price paid: the weakening of Isaiah's portentous calling with its terrible purpose and consequences. *Hina* has to be understood as purposeful and *mepote* as preventative. The only way of doing this and making sense is to understand the logion as indicating that God is determined to drive Israel without mercy into its contradictions and to prevent it at all costs from getting off the hook by a superficial act of repentance. This is the hardening thesis that Moses is described as having put forward in connection with Pharaoh's intransigence (Exod. 4.21; 7.3; 9.12, among others) and which Isaiah now develops in terms of Israel's. If Jesus used this same logion in connection with his ministry and in particular about his parable-making it surely follows that his concern was to heal people by driving them 'mercilessly' into facing up to their contradictions, with all the consequences that this entailed. I know of no persuasive evidence for doubting the originality of the Isaiah logion. Its multiple attestation and scandalous nature both make it likely that Jesus did indeed use it of himself. Some have suggested that it was added by the Church to explain the obduracy of the Jews (see Scott, *Hear Then*, p. 24, and Rom. 11.8).

If I am right we should see Jesus' concern in his parables as being with peoples' attitudes and behaviour rather than with their lack of spiritual or religious knowledge. This, as I see it, ties in with the picture projected by the rest of the Gospel material. I believe Jesus' practice was to use the eye-opening effect of parables to offer correction and possible relief to people whose attitudes were 'all screwed-up' and my principal concern in this book is to justify this *healing model*.

It is true that since the advent of modern scholarship most commentators, whether they have followed Dodd in believing that Jesus' parables were designed to tease the mind into active thought or have seen them rather as functioning like works of art, or even if as true conservatives they have continued to view them as allegories, have taken it as read that they had a twofold effect: to veil the realities they address as well as to reveal them. If this were really the case the parables of Jesus would be radically different from the three sorts I have described above, which all operate essentially as revelators. However, I am convinced that such a self-contradictory intent is just a figment of the imagination, which developed in the early church[33] only because Jesus' parables were preserved in such a poor state. This latter point will be discussed more fully in the next chapter.

Compacted Parables

In most parables, as in all similes, the subject and the illustration are kept rigorously apart. However, I have found at least one parabolic saying in the Rabbinic tradition which shows clear signs of compaction since its 'story' is made up of subject and illustrative components mixed together. Rabbi Simeon ben Lakish, living in the third century, spoke about a message that the Jews from Palestine sent to those living in Babylon, which went thus:

Let the bunches of grapes pray for the leaves.[34]

Simeon himself interpreted the message figuratively:[35]

However, nothing suggests that Jesus' compatriots were less obdurate before the crucifixion than after it.

33. Significantly as part of Mark's cult of mystery. See Drury, *Parables*, ch. 3.

34. Feldman, *Rabbis*, p. 130.

35. No one should be in the least bit surprised by this. One can take it as a rule that all reported parabolic sayings, in the form of logic-based stories isolated from their contexts, were *explained* allegorically since there was no alternative way of

> This nation is likened unto a vine. Its branches stand for the landowners;
> the cluster of grapes for the disciples of the wise; the leaves for the
> Amme-Ha'aretz; the rods or thin branches for the empty ones in Israel.

However, visualising it thus as an allegory one tends to lose sight of the
parabolic simile on which it was based, which would have gone like this:

As the bunches of grapes have a vital need that the vine remain healthy	So the disciples of the wise should pray for the common people (the *Amme-Ha'aretz*).

This is why I believe we should see this logion rather as a compacted
parable. What we have in this speech-mechanism is something rather
special: a metaphoric emphasis that has been added to a parable's concentrated illumination. It is this combination that gives compacted parables their typically directive characteristic, as if the speaker were pointing
his or her finger while delivering them. For this reason I call compacted
parables *instructive illuminations*.

You will notice that whereas parables are typically open-ended in that
they invite the interlocutors to draw their own conclusions, and whereas
allegories are fundamentally dogmatic in that they simply state a particular understanding of a situation on a take-it-or-leave-it basis, compacted
parables lie somewhere in between. Thus, like allegories, they make a
clear proclamation; like parables they function by comparison, by appeal
to awarenesses.

There are four parables that the evangelists have recorded which I
judge to be compacted (The Narrow Door, Treasure from the Storehouse, The Ploughman Who Looks Back and The Kindled Fire). It is
likely that Jesus would have used this speech-form in a particular way.
Whereas he would have used ordinary parables in market-place encounters to bring people to awareness, he would have used compacted parables in withdrawn or teaching situations when reminding his disciples of
what they had already seen and heard; so bringing certain lessons from
life to the forefront of their minds.

Proverbs

The only proverbs I am concerned with here are the two-dimensional
kind: those containing an illustration, like this:

> It hurts to kick against the goads. (Acts 26.14)

doing this apart from verbally reconstructing the background and incident, which
was extremely difficult.

Almost every simile is forgotten just as soon as it is produced. Only the odd one proves so apt that people start using it themselves and it becomes an integral part of the living language, like the example I gave about my daughter coming in from the rain like a wet rag. Exactly the same thing happens with parables. In the transference of such a choice parable from its first use into the community's culture its specific reference is lost and its significance generalized. Perhaps this was how proverbs such as the one above, as well as the two cited in the synoptic tradition,[36] came into being.

Acted Parables?

Jeremias ends his famous study of parables with a short section[37] in which he deals with what he calls Jesus' 'parabolic actions'. However, when one examines the deeds he refers to, in almost every case they turn out to be acted representations operating as assertions, which puts them on a par with the prophets' acted allegories.[38] So to call them parabolic is, on the understanding of parable that I propose, strictly erroneous.

For example Jeremias talks of Jesus' healings and rejection of fasting as *proclaiming* the Messianic Age; of Jesus's renaming of Simon as *designating* him the foundation stone of the eschatalogical Temple of God; of Jesus' entry into Jerusalem on a donkey as *symbolizing* the peaceful purpose of his mission and his cleansing of the temple as a *symbolic expression* of his royal authority.

He also cites the numerous occasions on which Jesus extended hospitality to the outcasts, and calls them 'prophetic signs' and 'silent proclamations'. I am most unhappy with this since it tends to detract from the intrinsic value of such conduct. The symbolic act of changing a person's name derives its power not from the act itself, which is comparatively trivial, but from the fact that it points towards something that is so much greater. An act of solidarity with an outcast, however, is a very different matter since here the primary significance is in the deed itself. The very same distinction holds true when you compare Jesus' decision to ride into Jerusalem on a donkey with, say, an act of healing.

36. See catalogue at end of Part I, p. 120 below.
37. Jeremias, *Parables*, pp. 227-29.
38. See p. 35 above.

Of course what we find in the Gospels is not just Jesus' behaviour but the way in which the early church viewed it. Thus Jeremias may have felt justified in speaking about Jesus' healings and his behaviour towards the outcasts as symbolic, since the early church clearly intended its readers to see that something more than just human solidarity was involved. However, this is to use the word 'symbolic' in a strange way for it does not mean what it usually does: that we should ignore the acts as acts and instead concentrate on their significance. It means something quite different: that we should not stop at the act itself but go on to pursue the questions that it raises.

To use the language of symbols in dealing, in one paragraph, with such diverse acts as Jeremias does is to invite confusion. But, even worse, to talk about them under the heading of 'Parables in Action' is to make confusion worse confounded.

I would like to illustrate the importance of making a distinction between representations and illustrations, when judging so-called 'acted parables'. Consider Jesus' breaking of the bread and sharing of the cup during the last supper. This act which, if Paul and Luke are correct, he intended to be perpetuated, contains three possible likenesses: wine as shed blood, broken bread as a broken body and the act of taking in food as accepting into your life what someone has done for you.

Had Jesus been performing an acted parable when he passed around the cup and bread and told his disciples to share them we would have to envisage him using these as awareness-bringing likenesses, much as he had used the 'magical' operation of yeast within the dough to open their eyes to the astonishing way in which the kingdom comes. However, to understand in these terms what Jesus was doing is to render it meaningless since there is nothing characteristic of wine or broken bread that can make us see something in the life and death of Jesus to which we might conceivably be blind.[39] Even if the process of eating food may seem an apt comparative for the way in which people take on board some

---

39. In view of their personal experiences of the Holy Communion some may find it very difficult to accept that Jesus' symbolic use of eating and drinking did not evoke in his disciples an original awareness such as that produced by one of his parables. This is because they fail to distinguish between the eternal freshness of a good *representation* with its ability, by means of an assertive *re-naming*, to gather together and bring to mind the pristine quality of awarenesses previously gained; and the brutal moment of an actual first-time *discovery* brought about by a powerful *illustration*.

profound truth, it is quite insufficient to explain the power one senses in this shared action.

Clearly, Jeremias is right in describing the distribution of the wine and the bread as 'the last symbolic act of Jesus' life' for only by seeing the connections wine/blood, bread/body, ingesting food/making yours what has come from elsewhere, *as symbols*, is their full power understood. Jesus was not opening his disciples' eyes to some awareness to which they had previously been blind. He was encapsulating his life, with all its significance, in these symbols and offering them to his followers as a repeatable celebration of all that he did, and was, for them.

The only deeds in Jeremias' list that he does not actually write of as symbolic (representative) are Jesus' setting a child in the midst of the disciples (Mk 9.33-36) and his washing of their feet (Jn 13.1-11). These are what I have termed *models* since they operate in one dimension only, there being nothing lying behind them to which they refer. Jeremias seems to disagree: he describes the latter as 'an example of the love that stooped to serve', the love that stoops to serve being an abstract generality and the washing of the feet the clarifying concrete example. However, as I have previously pointed out, I believe that the people of Jesus' day were unused to thinking in this way.

The fact that all of Jeremias's proposed examples of parabolic action prove to be nothing of the kind still leaves unanswered the question whether acted parables are a real possibility. As we saw, Isaiah and Ezekiel moved from allegorical words to allegorical deeds in order to increase the power of their assertions, since they felt that the people were no longer listening.[40] The question is whether parables as illuminations can be enhanced in a similar way.

The power of a parable depends on three factors: (1) the *thrust* of the likeness. (2) The inappropriateness of the likeness or *kick*. (3) The *gap* which focuses attention and invites participation and discovery. As far as I can see none of these are enhanced by turning words into deeds. Indeed, were you to try to act out a parable you would simply labour its attack and blunt its thrust. To achieve the desired end, the parable-maker needs to adopt a stand-back, throw-away style that leaves the opponent plenty of room to become implicated and so 'hang' him- or herself. Acted parables, being counter-productive, never developed.

40. Wilder considers these allegorical deeds to be acted parables, *Language*, p. 91. In doing so he shows the usual inability to distinguish between illustrations and representations. See Chapter 2 above.

Having now come to an end of this brief survey of two-dimensional speech-forms, I wish to make it clear that while my interest is specifically with parables there are good reasons why I have nonetheless analysed *all* the relevant two-dimensional speech-forms and their uses.

First, in the synoptic tradition we find Jesus' parables in a significantly damaged state—due both to the lost knowledge of their contexts (background and incident, in particular) and the evangelists' attempts to make sense of them in this atrophied condition. In this respect they resemble Jotham's parable (in which the ending is garbled). Had they been preserved for posterity as beautifully as David's unknown biographer preserved Nathan's parable, their form and usage would have been plain for all to see. However, the fact that they are impaired means that we are left in considerable doubt about these things. So, just as archaeologists must possess a wide knowledge of all the styles of ceramic art which have appeared over the centuries if they are to have a hope of correctly identifying the broken bits of pottery they have just dug up; so we are obliged to have a basic knowledge of all the various speech-forms that make up the general two-dimensional field, if we are to understand correctly what Jesus was reported as saying when he spoke 'in parables'.

This is made all the more necessary since most New Testament scholars use words like simile, metaphor, figure and allegory very loosely, and because there is as yet no general agreement as to what such words signify in connection with the parable debate. One of my preoccupations has therefore been to define them clearly and to be rigorous in the way I use them.

Secondly, it has been my concern to demonstrate, against Jeremias and the hold-all theorists, that parables, both biblical and unbiblical, ancient and modern, have a precise and ascertainable *form* and *function* so that when Jesus employed them, as the evangelists usually present him doing, in 'market-place' debates to bring about awarenesses and expose twisted attitudes, people would have been perfectly familiar with the device he was using. This would have been no less true because they had no precise word to describe it and were incapable of giving it a clear definition.

This is not to deny Jeremias's point that the Aramaic word for parable—*mathla*—was used very broadly. However, the fact that in first-century Palestine there were not different names for all the various speech-forms in use, let alone the different types of parable, does not mean that these did not exist. It only means that their users' approach was unanalytical.

There was no harm in being unanalytical just so long as you happened to be present when a parable was spoken. However, when it came to dealing with parables damaged during oral transmission the biblical writers' unanalytical approach seriously let them down. Because they did not appreciate how much of a parable's impact results from the proper functioning of its overall mechanism they failed to see the need to make a full reconstruction and instead concentrated all their attention on providing Jesus' stories with a satisfactory 'meaning'. In other words the parables' form and operation, already hard hit in oral transmission, were now completely sacrificed. It follows that we have to employ all our analytical skills if we are to sort out the confused situation the evangelists have left to us.

Thirdly, I have wished to make it clear that the specific characteristics of a speech-form determine, to a large extent, its usage. Figures and allegories, because of their natural assertiveness, are generally used to provide a personal interpretation of events on a take-it-or-leave-it basis. Similes, because of their simple likenesses, are generally used to produce descriptive illustrations. Metaphors, because of their compaction, are used to make emphatic illuminations. Parables, because of their pointed 'logics', are used to make concentrated illuminations. I have insisted on this, because Dodd and Jeremias commonly make out that Jesus used parables for purposes for which they were entirely unsuited: as assertions, exhortations or condemnations.

Three simple distinctions should be kept firmly in mind in order to successfully work out how these various speech-forms operate.

Take the distinction between *representations* and *illustrations*. The fact is that in our common speech we can use these words interchangeably. For example, we can speak of an artist's picture as a representation or an illustration of its subject, meaning much the same thing. However, in this exercise it is important to maintain the distinction, against the rather relaxed usage: a representation is a one-stands-for-another relation and an illustration is a one-like-another relation.

Exactly the same point holds true for the distinction I have drawn between *models* and *examples* in that in casual usage they are easily confused. However, for our strict purposes models are one-dimensional: behaviour taken from life to be followed or avoided; whereas examples are two-dimensional: concrete instances of abstract generalities.

It is also easy to confuse what I have called the *kick* and the *gap* since both produce a marked effect. However, they are quite different, the one causing a pleasurable sense of inappropriateness and the other an unbalancing interruption leading to discovery. So take care to distinguish these two!

Before concluding this chapter it is necessary to tackle one further subject crucial to the parable debate: how far it is possible to fuse two speech-forms together. In practice this means combining representations with illustrations since, as I have already pointed out, the biblical writers seldom if ever used instances.

In answering this question I shall pick up something I said earlier about the basic incompatibility of representations and illustrations,[41] which stems from the fact that representations are essentially *identifications* whereas illustrations are essentially likenesses based on *distinctions*. What I was calling attention to is the consideration that just as it is impossible to drive a car in two gears at the same time so it is impossible to read a phrase as a representation and an illustration at the same time. Take this saying of Hosea:

> My people inquire of a thing of wood, and their staff gives them
> oracles.
> For a spirit of harlotry has led them astray, and they have left
> their God to play the harlot. (4.12)

There are two ways in which readers may understand how 'harlotry' is used here. Either they may take it as a metaphor (illustration), in which case their minds appreciate what is being said as an illumination intended to open peoples' eyes; as if the prophet were saying 'Don't you see that in worshipping foreign gods you are acting like harlots?' Or they may take it as a figure (representation) in which case their minds read 'harlot' basically as a short and convenient way of talking about what we would call ideological/theological betrayal. Here the prophet is simply putting forward his opinion that in worshiping idols Israel is betraying everything that made it what it is.

I emphasize that I am talking about how one reads the text and not the intention of the writer. Sometimes the latter actually specifies the way in which he or she wants to be understood:

> So the Lord cut off from Israel head and tail, palm branch and reed in one
> day—the elder and honored man is the head, and the prophet who teaches

41. p. 42 above.

lies is the tail; for those who lead this people lead them astray, and those
who are led by them are swallowed up. (Isa. 9.14-16)

Here there is no dichotomy for the readers are told to take the text
figuratively, with head signifying elders, tail representing prophets, palm
branch a symbol for leaders and reed standing for the led. However, in
most cases the text is ambiguous and it is up to the readers to make the
choice. Of course they may well hesitate and try one way first and then
the other, but in doing so they will be conscious of 'changing gear'.

In the absence of a clear indication from the author, the readers will
be much influenced as to which way to take a particular ambiguous
speech-form: by its novelty or otherwise. Thus the first time that a
prophet refers to Israel as a harlot it is certain to hit the readers between
the eyes and they will automatically accept it as an illumination. However, the more often the prophet makes the reference the more its
impact on the readers will fade and the chances of their reading it
figuratively, that is, as shorthand for a rather complex set of circumstances about which the prophet has definite ideas, will increase.

Indeed this may well be the way in which figures are developed.
Someone starts off by comparing a hierarchical community to a
countryside in which both palm trees and reeds abound. The simile
sticks in peoples' minds and through use is strengthened into a
metaphor. However, constant repetition dulls it. Now, with most if not
all of its illumination emptied, others may continue to employ it as a
convenient and colourful way of talking about such a community when
expressing opinions on other things.

This would seem to suggest that there may be occasions when the
basic incompatibility of representations and illustrations is overcome. For
with the repeated use of the same metaphor in an extended text, as the
mind adjusts from understanding it purely as an illustration to reading it
more and more as a representation, readers become adept at switching
between the two modes of thought. Thus, in the mid-period, it can
almost seem to them as if they were reading the text both ways at the
same time.

You can verify this for yourself by reading the extended allegory in
Ezekiel 16. The prophet starts out with what looks like a powerful
metaphor of Israel as the girl child abandoned at birth on a Palestinian
hillside. At this point his intention may appear to be to open people's
eyes to Israel's act of betrayal. However, as his speech progresses, this
apparent metaphor and its apparent illuminative quality become

swamped by repetition and readers find themselves with an allegorical story in which the basic intention of the prophet seems to be to lay out a special understanding of Israel's history. People like ourselves, who are strangers to the situation of Ezekiel and his hearers, may be inclined to read a transition from metaphor to allegory into his text. But this would be a mistake, as I will try to explain.

In the portering department of the hospital where I work we do not use allegories but we do give each other nicknames. These, too, are representations and so operate much like allegories. One of my mates is called 'The Head Porter'. He is not the head porter, but he knows everything that is going on in the department and is always telling the real head porter and myself, his deputy, what to do—much to our irritation.

In calling him 'The Head Porter' we are not trying to draw peoples' attention to the fact that he acts like a head porter for we use the appellation only amongst ourselves and we know perfectly well what he is like. For us he is not *like* a head porter he *is* 'The Head Porter': the 'is' indicating not the presence of a metaphor but the fact that our calling him thus is symbolic not comparative. It indicates that we are using an 'in' language, sharing a joke; that we are not *describing him* but *celebrating together* his special presence amongst us and getting pleasure from it.[42]

Of course those new in the department who did not understand what was going on might hear my friend being talked about as 'The Head Porter' and, witnessing his behaviour, say to themselves: 'It's true he does act like a head porter'. But in understanding the title thus, as an illustration, the newcomers would not be sharing our celebration. Only on becoming members of the in-group would they begin to realize our true intention in naming my friend thus.

The same thing is true of our appreciation of the allegories of the prophets. We are inclined to read them first as illustrations: as metaphor

---

42. Note the previous discussion on the bread and wine in the last supper, p. 74 above. There may be some difficulty in seeing this point because we do not make much of the distinction between a likeness in an illustration and an appropriateness in a representation, tending to call both 'likenesses' indiscriminately. So we have to make an effort to see the real difference between a true likeness, which involves a comparison and is intended to be enlightening, and a 'likeness' in a nickname. With the latter there is no comparison and the only intention is to enjoy the appropriateness and the incongruity of the new name given to a subject whose real character, all agree, is only too familiar.

rather than figure. But this is only because, as newcomers to the situation, we do not properly appreciate the language of an in-group. We have therefore to learn, that in talking about Israel as the harlot who is always running after foreign lovers, Ezekiel is sharing with his compatriots the perverse enjoyment of this extended nickname.

So much for the notion of allegories being 'kick-started' by metaphors. In the case of parables the argument for the possibility of fusing together illustrative and representative speech-forms is somewhat different. Here the suggestion is that in starting out with a basic illustrative story, the author seeks to indicate the subject of his discourse (the parable's application) by including one or more figurative pointers in his story. For example, a master = God, a harvest = the parousia, an accounting = the last judgment. Since the evangelists clearly used this 'clue-symbol' approach it is hardly surprising that most commentators follow in their footsteps.

However, you have only to state the proposition thus baldly to see what a misconceived idea it is. In the first place, to be effective as a concentrated illumination a parable story has to be constructed so that it contains nothing that can distract from its logic. Yet here we are talking about the inclusion of a number of elements the sole purpose of which is to point the listener in a completely different direction.

In the second place it is not as if the parable-makers were starved of alternative ways of letting listeners know what they were talking about. As I have said, in most cases the problem would not even have existed, seeing that the subject of the parable would have been the topic that Jesus and his hearers were already discussing. But even if this were not the case, it would have been the most natural thing in the world for him to start off by introducing the subject and then telling his story.

Indeed, if anyone ever did tell a parable in the way suggested above one would be forced to conclude that he was intent on obscuring his own illumination: turning on a searchlight and then throwing a blanket over it; or, as Jesus himself put it, lighting a lamp and then shoving it under the bed!

Chapter 5

THE CASE FOR RECONSTRUCTION

It is well understood now that the evangelists were not writing history and that they all used their sources with a degree of freedom that most present-day historians would not. However, this of itself cannot account for the many inconsistencies and even bizarre features which prevent their versions of the parables from being perceived as down-to-earth comments that are perfectly clear. I am therefore obliged to postulate that either the evangelists were struggling with damaged material and were doing their best to use it in a meaningful way which would not betray their master, or they were well in control of material they knew to be bizarre and inconsistent in the first place. Those who take the former position see the need to reconstruct the parables, whereas those who take the latter do not.

The Argument against Reconstruction

It has been suggested that since Julicher all major commentators have adopted the line that the Gospel parables need to be abstracted from their context and subjected to a certain amount of reconstructive work before they can be properly appreciated.[1] However, conservative scholarship has never gone along with the reconstructionists' primary contention that allegory has no place within parables.

Blomberg
Craig Blomberg, for example, draws attention to certain errors in the work of Dodd and Jeremias. In particular he argues that the synoptic parables should be read along with those of the rabbis (which he takes as being allegorical) and points out that it is far-fetched to claim, as Jeremias does, that Jesus' approach was something quite new.[2]

---

1. Drury, *Parables*, p. 1.
2. Blomberg, *Interpreting*, p. 58.

He also rightly states that there is no justification for the way in which the Julicher/Jeremias tradition denigrates allegory as 'an inferior art form'.[3] He argues that allegories can be as simple and concrete as any illustrative story and that it is foolish to pretend that there are not limits set within them which control the number of derivative meanings one can properly extract.[4] He does not deny that the early church exegetes went over the top in trying to find meaning for every detail in the parable stories but makes the valid point that this in itself is no proof that the parables were not allegories. I personally would add that allegories are no different from illustrative stories in this respect, for these too can be pushed too far.

Blomberg also disputes the well-known contention that it is the multiplicity of points of comparison that distinguish a parable from an allegory.[5] Here I find myself in agreement with his conclusion, although not with his reasoning since he goes on to argue that parables make more than one point. This I believe to be a serious mistake for the essential nature of parable is such that every element is selected solely with a view to building the 'logic' which creates the overall thrust. This said, I am perfectly willing to agree that most biblical allegories share this 'single mindedness' and so in this respect are indistinguishable from parables.

However, it must be pointed out that in his main purpose—to prove that parables are allegories—Blomberg is quite unconvincing. Indeed he only manages to make some sort of a case by studiously ignoring the fundamental distinction between representative and illustrative speech-forms: the very basis of the difference between allegories and parables. For example he writes:

> The only really close biblical parallel [to Jesus' parables] is Nathan's story of the ewe lamb (2 Sam. 12.1-10)—and it, incidentally, is given at least a partially allegorical explanation (the rich man represents David, the poor man is Uriah, and the sheep stands for Bathsheba).[6]

It is quite mistaken to say that the rich man *represents* David. It is certainly true that they are in a sense 'equivalents', for, as Bultmann pointed out,[7] when you illustrate a relationship between two things, *a*

3.   Blomberg, *Interpreting*, pp. 41-42.
4.   Blomberg, *Interpreting*, p. 52.
5.   Blomberg, *Interpreting*, pp. 52-53.
6.   Blomberg, *Interpreting*, p. 48.
7.   Bultmann, *History*, p. 198.

and *b*, there have to be two complementary items *a'* and *b'*, in the similitude. Consequently you should expect to find a certain number of such equivalences in any parable. But this is quite different from saying that in reading Nathan's parable you should substitute David for the rich man. To do so would simply ruin the illustration since this depends on seeing David (in life) and the rich man (in the story) as distinct individuals who are *alike* in abusing their power.

It is true that when David said 'As the Lord lives, the man who has done this deserves to die', Nathan replied '*You* are the man'; this looks superficially as if he wanted David to see the man in the story as a representation. However, it was necessary for Nathan to indicate the subject of the parable in this way because he had purposely disguised his parable as a case for the king to judge. All he meant by his answer was 'Make no mistake, this story is about *you*, O King!' It is nonsensical to suppose that he meant 'For the rich man read yourself, for the poor man read Uriah and for the sheep read Bathsheba', because it was not Bathsheba but Uriah who was murdered. In any case, to introduce such figurative (verbal symbolic) references would have destroyed the parable's thrust.

Being blind to this distinction between representations and illustrations Blomberg believes he can reinforce his argument that Jesus' parables were allegorical by pretending that their nearest relatives—the parables of the rabbis—were also allegorical.[8] But as Bultmann showed long ago, what people take for allegorical features in the stories of the rabbis are usually nothing of the kind.[9] Indeed my impression is that people only suspect the presence of allegory because where the 'logic' is weak an air of contrivance is imparted to the whole story:

> There are three kinds of nuts. The *Pereh* (soft-shelled eatable) nuts, nuts
> of a medium hardness, and *Kitron* (a species of hard) nuts: the *Pereh* nut
> which bursts open of itself, the medium nut which breaks when beaten,
> and the hard nut which is difficult to break, and which even when cracked
> by means of a stone is of no use at all. Even so it is with the Israelites.
> There are some among them who do good of their own accord. These are
> the soft nuts. There are others who, when solicited for a good cause, give
> readily. These are the medium ones. And there are others again, who even
> when urged to do a good deed are appealed to in vain.[10]

---

8.   Although the surviving parables of the rabbis are all of a later date than those of Jesus I see no reason to dispute their close relationship.

9.   Bultmann, *History*, p. 198.

10.   Feldman, *Rabbis*, p. 178. See also *The King and his Vineyard*, p. 66 above.

There is a handful of genuine parables from the rabbis that contain allegorical elements but they are second-rate affairs since the insertion of figurative elements quite spoils them as illustrations:

> For whose sake was it that the Holy One, blessed be He, revealed himself in Egypt? It was for the sake of Moses...

> R[abbi] Nissim said: This might be compared to a priest who had a garden of figs with a place therein which was declared to be ritually unclean. Being desirous of eating some figs, he said to someone, 'Go, and tell the [tenant] that the owner of the garden has ordered thee to bring him two figs.' He went and told him thus. Whereupon the [tenant] replied: 'What care I for the owner of the garden? Get thee to thy work.' Then said the priest unto him: 'I shall go myself into the garden.' 'But thou wilt be going into an unclean place', they objected. And he replied: 'Even though there be 100 grades of uncleanliness, yet I shall go thither, so that my messenger shall not be put to shame.'[11]

You sense a thrust within this story but you have to search for it. In trying to make certain that his audience will understand the comparison he is driving at, Rabbi Nissim takes the envoy out of the final conversation with the priest, substituting 'they' as the interlocutors, so that he may then refer to him as 'my messenger' a well-known appellation for a prophet. In other words he clarifies the subject of his parable for his listeners by allegorizing the story.

Why does he do this? Well, his problem is that the natural ending to his story would have been that the priest agreed to go into an unclean place to make sure that the tenant's insubordination did not pay off.[12] This means that he has to work hard to pull the story round so that it focuses on the priest's feelings for his messenger. But the tactic he employs, referring the listeners to the special relationship between God and his prophets, involves allegorizing the story, which simply makes everything worse. The only way he could have carried things off would have been to insist on the special relationship between the priest and his messenger *in the story*, by describing him not just as 'someone' but, say, as 'a dear friend' and then writing the final conversation as taking place between these two people.

To understand what I mean by the distinction between representations and illustrations, which Blomberg is unwilling to recognize, you have only to look at this magnificent allegorical exchange:

11. Feldman, *Rabbis*, pp. 39-40.
12. Cf. *The Rebellious Tenants*, Pb. 13, p. 143 below.

R[abbi] Eleazar bar Simon. . . was appointed by the Roman Government
as chief of the body-guard or executioner, and being rebuked by R[abbi]
Joshua b[en] Korah with the stinging remark: 'O, Vinegar, son of wine,
how long wilt thou deliver the people of our God unto slaughter?', he
answered in excuse of his conduct: 'I am only destroying the thorns out of
the vineyard.' To which R[abbi] Joshua rejoined: 'Let the owner of the
vineyard himself. . . come and destroy the thorns out of the vineyard.'[13]

When Joshua says to Eleazar 'O, Vinegar, son of wine' he means of
course 'You treacherous Israelite'. He adopts the well-known usage in
which the vineyard, the vine or even the wine is taken as a representative figure for Israel and extends it by making 'vinegar' stand for an
Israelite gone sour. Similarly, when Eleazar replies 'I am only destroying
the thorns out of the vineyard', he means 'I am only executing bad
Israelites'; the vineyard now representing Israel and the thorns within it
individuals who are counterproductive. Again, when Joshua answers
'Let the owner of the vineyard himself come and destroy the thorns' he
means 'dealing with bad Israelites is God's work not yours.' The owner,
as in most rabbinic figures, represents God. Of course you *could* take
Joshua to be saying to Eleazar 'You are *like* wine that has turned sour'
but this would be to reduce a bitingly powerful indictment to an insipid
comparison.

It is important to realize that by understanding the 'story' elements in
these remarks as representations rather than likenesses one sees their
power as being developed in a specific way. Here the impact is produced by a combination of the meaning and associations carried by the
chosen representations (wine being Israel and vinegar being unpalatable,
for example) and the force of the individual's authoritative understanding of events; each rabbi is clearly making much of the fact that this is
how *he* sees things and you can take it or leave it.

With parables, on the other hand, the power of the logion is generated
by the way in which all the elements in the story-dimension combine in
a logic to produce the thrust. Of course, all illustrations work on the
thrust principle but in parable the illustration is particularly extended and
the thrust concentrated. This is a very simple yet certain way of distinguishing parable from allegory which I recommend to Blomberg. Using
it one can say with absolute certainty that the following rabbinic sayings
are parables, and good ones at that:

13. Feldman, *Rabbis*, p. 134.

When the shepherd is lame it is then that the sheep run away.
At the gate of the fold there are words (bargaining), but at the stalls
(where the [pregnant] sheep are delivered) there is strict account.

[There was] a lamb whom the wolf came to carry away. The shepherd set
himself in pursuit in order to rescue it from the mouth of the wolf.
Between the shepherd and the wolf the lamb was torn.[14]

Indeed the thrust of this last saying is even better appreciated when one
knows that it was used by Rabbi Judah Halevi to explain the somewhat
mixed feelings of the Israelites when Moses' efforts to free them from
the Egyptians simply resulted in the screw being turned down on them
even more (Exod. 5.21).

Because Blomberg will not admit to this difference between representative and illustrative stories his definitions appear quite inadequate.
Quoting Madeleine Boucher with approval he says that 'Allegory is
nothing more and nothing less than *an extended metaphor in narratory
form*'.[15] Thus for him the only parables that are not allegories are those
which are too short to be narrative and which, in his words, are 'simple
comparisons rather than full-fledged narratives'. The logic here is that
metaphors are simple comparisons, and allegories are extended narrative
comparisons.

However, if one means by allegory simply a narrative comparison
then of course all parables are allegories since, as we have seen, parables
are by nature complex. But by defining things in this way one loses possession of a perfectly good word; why bother to call stories 'parables' if
they are really allegories? Worse still, we then have to coin a new word,
for how else are we going to distinguish between stories built on
representations and those built on illustrations?

The New Hermeneutic
It is not only conservatives who have hesitations about reconstructing
parables. Followers of the new hermeneutic have also persistently
argued against Julicher, Dodd and Jeremias that the important thing is not
to find out what the parables *meant* to those who first heard them but
what they *mean* to Christians today.

They make the point that we can never be certain the evangelists have
adequately recorded the situation which gave rise to a particular parable
and that in many cases the evangelists have not made any attempt in this

14. Feldman, *Rabbis*, pp. 225, 215
15. Blomberg, *Interpreting*, p. 43.

direction at all. They conclude that the original meaning of any given parable is at best in question and at worst beyond recall.[16] This is why they place all their emphasis on the hermeneutical aspect of parable study while cautioning those, like myself, who want to adopt a reconstructional approach.

Drury

John Drury develops this doubt, first voiced by Crossan, about the possibility of making viable reconstructions of the parables since 'we have literally no language and no parables of Jesus except and insofar as such can be retrieved and reconstructed from within the language of their earliest interpreters'.[17] His thesis is that 'A parable by Jesus cannot be restored without constant reference to unassailably genuine work by Jesus' and 'This necessary criterion we do not have'. He likens the reconstructionist critic to a 'restorer trying to clean an allegedly over-painted canvas by Rubens without having access to a single indisputably authentic Rubens painting or even sketch'.[18]

In other words, Drury believes that to try to reconstruct the parables of Jesus is a waste of time and that we should occupy ourselves with the evangelists' allegorized parables instead. He maintains that we should read the synoptic parables, especially those of Mark, along with Ezekiel's typically fabulous and surreal *meshalim*,[19] and therefore understand them as intrinsically allegorical and riddle-like: as puzzling, incongruous, bizarre and nonsensical.[20]

The basic flaw in this position is that in fact nothing could be less like Ezekiel's *meshalim* than the gospel parables since there is not a single 'logic'-based story in the former and not a single 'logicless' story in the latter. I can demonstrate my point by examining, on each side, the stories which seem most likely to break this rule:

The only *mashal* in Ezekiel that looks as if it might be logic-based is the one about the wood of the vine:

> Son of Man, how does the wood of the vine surpass any wood, the vine branch which is among the trees of the forest? Is wood taken from it to make anything? Do men take a peg from it to hang any vessel on? Lo, it is

16. Funk, *Hermeneutic*, p. 149; Via, *Parables*, pp. 21-22.
17. Drury, *Parables*, pp. 2-3.
18. Drury, *Parables*, p. 3.
19. Drury, *Parables*, pp. 10-11.
20. Drury, *Parables*, pp. 44-45, 58.

given to the fire for fuel; when the fire has consumed both ends of it, and
the middle of it is charred, is it useful for anything? Behold, when it was
whole, it was used for nothing; how much less, when the fire has consumed it and it is charred, can it ever be used for anything? (Ezek. 15.2-4)

This appears to parallel a synoptic logion: As there is nothing quite as
useless as salt that has lost its taste, so there is nothing quite as useless as
the wood of the vine—especially when half burnt! However, this is to
ignore the logic in the idea of salt *that has lost its taste* and the absence
of such a logic in the vine-wood story. Of course I could easily provide
the latter with a logic by expanding it to talk of the vine that has *ceased
to produce fruit*. But that is not how Ezekiel frames his story. He characteristically presents it as an allegory; an assertion of his take-it-or-leave-
it understanding that among the surrounding nations Israel is of little
account and will be even less so when God has finished with it. So there
is no formal similarity between Ezekiel's vine-wood *mashal* and the
synoptic salt parable at all.

On the other hand, there is a logion from Mark that looks as if it
might be a logicless parable:

> There is nothing outside a man which by going into him can defile him;
> but the things which come out of a man are what defile him. Do you not
> see that whatever goes into a man from outside cannot defile him, since it
> enters, not his heart but his stomach, and so passes on... What comes out
> of a man is what defiles a man. (Mk 7.15-20)

There is no 'logic' here because there is nothing connecting the fact that
food which we take in does not sully, whereas faeces which we excrete,
do. Consequently if this saying had been used as a likeness—for example
to the things we hear as opposed to the things we say—it would have
lacked punch. But Mark does not present it (at least in the beginning) as
a likeness or a two-dimensional saying, which makes it curious that he
should call it a parable. That said, there is no question here of anything
allegorical so, in spite of the fact that Mark makes out that Jesus is being
mysterious, a formal comparison of even this logion with Ezekiel's
mashal is out of the question.

Drury does recognize that Jesus' parables, especially those from Luke,
differ from the *meshalim* of Ezekiel in being 'more realistic'.[21] But this
is an entirely secondary matter since realism is not a formal requisite of
logic-based parables. This is amply demonstrated by the story of the

---

21. See Coggin and Houlden, *Dictionary*, pp. 509-11.

donkey in which one's awareness that donkeys do not talk in no way prevents one from accepting the parable's logic. So in centring attention on the realistic aspect while ignoring the business of the logic Drury is seriously misled.

One other way in which Drury shows that he is mistaken in thinking that the Gospel parables are intrinsically allegorical riddles is that he talks about them as 'resorting to the absurd'.[22] He is right to say that the absurd is a feature of many of Jesus' parables, but that is not in the least bit surprising since there are only two basic ways of creating an adequate logic. One is by implying that something is obviously so, the other that it obviously is not so and that it would be *absurd* to believe it is. In other words the clear indication within a story that something is to be seen as absurd demonstrates the presence of a 'logic' and not of a 'logicless' riddle.

Because Drury fails to understand what is entailed by the fact that all of Jesus' stories, with the exception of the mythical account of the unclean spirit (Mt. 12.43; Lk. 11.24), are 'logic'-based, he can turn a blind eye to the evangelists' clear mistreatment of them. So he sees no reason to start afresh and try to reconstruct the parables in ways more appropriate to this their central feature.

However, what neither Drury, Blomberg nor the exponents of the new hermeneutic seem to appreciate is that once you realize that the evangelists have falsified (although, of course, in good faith) the basis of the parable—the story's 'logic'—you are forced to attempt a reconstruction or abandon all pretence of being interested in the historical Jesus.

The Reconstructional Approach

The first priority for the reconstructionist is to understand the process of decay. Why did the Gospel-writers treat Jesus' parables so badly? Before these had even come into their possession a natural process of disintegration would have already commenced. At best, memory of the parables' backgrounds, incidents and consequences would have become blurred (or more likely lost) and inevitably a certain amount of explanatory allegorization would have been laid over them. So not all the blame can be attributed to the evangelists.

They must nonetheless carry some responsibility. Their primary

22. Drury, *Parables*, pp. 46-48, 58, 63.

concern was not with Jesus' technique of parable-making any more than with his other arts of healing. This meant that they probably felt justified in sacrificing anything that remained of this aspect of the parabolic material in order to further their much more important theological design. After all, they were not writing Jesus' biography.

Unfortunately, in giving themselves such latitude they inadvertently gave to those who have come after them a false impression of what Jesus was doing when he spoke in parables. This means that if we are to rectify their fault we have to try to undo some of their work as well as that of those who preceded them. This in turn means understanding the whole process by which parables were transmitted.

Parables, like exotic fruit, are intrinsically difficult to preserve and begin to disintegrate almost as soon as they have been delivered. This presumably is why logic-based stories are so rare in the Hebrew Bible. The survival of Jotham's and Nathan's stories shows that parable-making goes back a long way and perhaps was in the culture before Israel's beginning. However, the only other sign of their presence in the rest of the Hebrew scriptures is a few broken bits and pieces, like Isaiah's stories of the axe and the earthen vessel which strove with their makers (10.15; 45.9); or his reference to the ploughman, the sower and the thresher (28.23-28); or Jeremiah's encounter with a potter who was dissatisfied with the work he had done (18.1-4).

Indeed, the presence of Nathan's denunciation as the only 'logic'-based story preserved in the Hebrew Bible in anything like its entirety requires some explaining. If 2 Samuel 1–10 is an account of an actual historical event, one of the reasons why it survived so well is undoubtedly the fact that it concerned what Israel's intellectual leadership believed was the crucial political question of the day: should Israel have a king and, if so, how should he behave?

A second reason may be that the parable was told in court, the only place in the community where there were people equipped to record it. A third reason could be the intrinsic drama of its setting: a story of sex implicating the king, a political cover-up involving the murder of a senior military leader, a scene of denunciation before the whole court, an unlikely climb down by the king and finally the mysterious death of the illegitimate child! If any parable were to find itself recorded it would surely be this one.

However, these factors would not have been what ultimately decided the parable's fate. It is possible to be so taken up with the genius of the inventors of parables that one rarely, if ever, considers what it takes to preserve them for posterity. Recording parables is a high art, far beyond the possibilities of most people even today, despite our much more sophisticated techniques. If it is still possible to appreciate the significance of Nathan's story, it may be because it has been written as if by an eye-witness. Whether or not this was actually the case, the writer was clearly a literary giant whose work is unrivalled in all the literature of the ancient Near East. He recounted the events of the time with such consummate skill that one feels as if one had been present oneself.

Most parables were not lucky enough to fall into such good hands. If there was nobody present who was capable of recording them when they were spoken, which we must suppose was generally the case, then they would only survive by being repeated from one person to another.

Decay of the Incident and Consequences

In the first stages of such transmission the story and background would hold up pretty well since stories, being carefully structured, are easily remembered and backgrounds are the common property of everyone living in the same time and place. (All Israelites would have been well aware of the kingship debate and realized its significance for a proper understanding of Nathan's story.) The consequences, however, would easily be left out of the account if they were not particularly spectacular but, more importantly, the details of the incident would start to be lost, not because they were thought unimportant but simply because people find it difficult to remember such things accurately.

The trouble is that with the disintegration of a parable's incident and consequences the purpose of the parable-maker in telling it is lost. Take for example the case of the parable of the donkey. From Peter Nieswand's report it looks as if the story should be classified as a *learner parable*; as if the Pakistani tribesman was simply offering his interlocutor a lesson. Personally, I think this was unlikely to have been the case but we cannot be sure since Nieswand has not provided us with an adequate description of the incident. All he mentions is the question concerning the loyalty of the Pakistani people and, since he ignores how the interlocutor reacted to the story, we really cannot tell how to take the parable at all.

However, I suspect that the interlocutor was one of Nieswand's fellow reporters and the Pakistani tribesman, irritated by this comfortable well-fed European's ignorance of how ordinary third-world people felt, decided to show him up for asking a damnfool question. Perhaps the reporter was so thick-skinned that he did not realize what was happening and simply took the parable to be a quaint bit of native culture that his readers back home would enjoy! Unfortunately we shall never know for when I tried to contact Peter Nieswand I sadly found that he had died.

When a parable incident disintegrates, the story comes to be seen no longer as referring to a particular person's attitude or problem, and so tends to be interpreted as teaching a lesson in the general terms defined by the background. Supposing we knew nothing about the actual circumstances surrounding Nathan's parable and all that was left was a vague understanding that it had something to do with the kingship debate. Were this the case we would probably wrongly infer that the parable had been designed to make the ideological 'point' that in Israel the king was not justified in using his powers to get what he wanted at the expense of his weaker subjects.

Decay of the Background

The incident is not the only casualty of the passage of time. If a parable survives in the collective memory even its background may become outdated. If this happens then all trace of the subject disappears and the story becomes effectively isolated. At this point the parable, if it is not too long and complicated, may become a proverb: a pithy teaching applicable to a host of similar situations.

Decay of the Story

At almost any moment in a parable's history someone is likely to come along and alter the story in one way or another. This is especially true when an editor decides to use it in a written text. It may be that the parable's thrust has been damaged by the loss of the incident or background, and the reporter is simply trying to make sense of it; or it may be that, as a result of the editor's own preoccupations, he or she has tried to squeeze more out of it than its maker intended.

Possibly both these things are true in the case of Jotham's parable (Judg. 9:8-15). It is most unlikely that it was told in quite the circumstances that the Hebrew Bible describes. There is, indeed, no reason to doubt the description of what took place after Gideon's death: dynastic rivalry and the action of Abimelech in stealing a march on his half-brothers by persuading his mother's people of Shechem to make him their king. But the tone of the parable, as it must have been originally, is nothing like a prophetic cry of defiance from the lips of a young man whose family has just been destroyed, even though this is how the book of Judges portrays it.

As I have previously pointed out, the story's present ending betrays the thrust it has been building to. The trees want a king to reign over them. First they ask the worthy candidates (the olive and the fig), but these refuse because it would mean giving up so much. So the trees ask a worthless candidate (the bramble), who promptly agrees. The thrust is painfully obvious: Of course the bramble is going to agree since as a worthless fellow he has nothing to lose!

But the way in which the biblical editor finishes the story is quite different:

> And the bramble said to the trees, 'If in good faith you are anointing me king over you, then come and take refuge in my shade; but if not, let fire come out of the bramble and devour the cedars of Lebanon.' (Judg. 9.15)

It is clear that at this point the story has been allegorized since it is no longer about all the different trees but about the 'cedars of Lebanon' (a symbolic reference to Israel) and because in the natural terms of the story it is nonsense to suggest that such trees can take refuge in the shade of a bramble bush. Furthermore it is really not too difficult to work out what some editor has been up to. He clearly wants the reader to see the parable in the light of Gideon's refusal to become Israel's king, which has just been described:

> Then the men of Israel said to Gideon, 'Rule over us, you and your son and your grandson also; for you have delivered us out of the hand of Midian.' Gideon said to them, 'I will not rule over you, and my son will not rule over you; the Lord will rule over you.' (Judg. 8.22-23)

In other words, the editor's aim is to use the story to underline the thesis that kingship is not compatible with Israel's beliefs and ideology. However, the parable does not make such a 'point'. Its impact at its original telling would have been more down to earth: *the trouble about the kingship is that only worthless people can be persuaded to do such an uncreative job.* It seems likely that such a parable would have come from one of the prophetic schools. However, recording it as such would have made it useless for the editor's purpose; therefore, perhaps he put it into the mouth of Jotham and changed its ending so that it made the desired point?

Though a number of parable-allegorizations in the Bible or the works of the rabbis are possibly the result of such a conscious manipulation by a later editor, it would be a mistake to try to account for the majority of them in this way. In all probability most allegorizations stem quite simply from the natural difficulties encountered in explaining parables *post eventum*. This, as we will see later in this chapter, was a very tricky exercise, as few scholars adequately appreciate.

In fact it would seem that in most cases the only practical way for a reporter to explain a parable with even a modicum of success was to find some way to allegorize it. This means that the presence of an allegorized parable either in the Gospels or in the Talmud and Midrashim cannot be taken as proof that the writers themselves understood the parables allegorically. It may only indicate the difficulty of transmitting their significance. Allegorization was probably the recognized way in which parables were reported.

There is, however, a further complication: the difficulty in determining in any given case what is an allegorization and what constitutes a genuine feature of the 'story'. For example, Hans Weder argues that the so-called allegorical interpretations of the Gospel parables are not really such but are simply the result of an application of the parables to experience.[23] This appears to be his way of talking about reporters' explanations. In my understanding even such well-intentioned transformations constitute allegorization, there being no formal way of distingushing them from other possibly less welcome manipulations.

More seriously, scholars like Scott and Drury have highlighted the unusual and absurd aspects of certain New Testament parables, such as the massive quantity of flour that a woman uses in her baking (Pb. 24), or the exaggerated multiplications of seed that are reported in the parable of The Sower (Pb. 7). They claim these features are original to the parables in that they are precisely what make such stories worth telling.

This is a point on which I fundamentally take issue with them. What neither Scott nor Drury appears to realize is that although such aspects may add to the attractiveness of the stories *as literature*, they would have destroyed them *as parabolic eye-openers delivered in the heat of a market-place encounter*. One can easily imagine a straightforward little

23. See D. Wenham, review of H. Weder, *Die Gleichnisse Jesus als Metaphern*, *JSNT* 14 (1982), p. 119.

story being used to effect by an opposition spokesman at Prime Minister's Question Time whereas one dependent on bizarre or unrealistic details would only serve to discredit the speaker in such circumstances. The fact is that in 'market-place' stories the shock is not produced by their quirky aspects but by the unexpected introduction of the stories themselves. The speaker then uses this tool to hold the audience in riveted attention until the final moment when the logic is delivered. The new hermeneutic's insistence on the importance of literary criticism can be dangerous rather than helpful. It is not literary criticism we need when dealing with parables, but a greater understanding of spoken communication.

That said, Drury rightly claims that these features which (superficially at least) approximate a certain number of Jesus' reported parables to the strange stories of the prophet Ezekiel, constitute allegorizations; he is able to do this, of course, because he makes no distinction between parable and allegory. As I see it, these features have to be termed allegorizations since they are figurative elements which, in their own right, point the listener in a predetermined direction regardless of the story's logic. But they are not only allegorizations. They are also out of place because in fulfilling their function they actually distract attention from the story's 'logic', the motor of the parabolic thrust. It cannot be emphasized enough that any feature in a parable that does not justify its place in building this 'logic' is *ipso facto* extraneous.

One further point that I believe counts against these bizarre features is the fact that there are many parables which contain none. I believe it is much easier to explain why it is that such features have been added— figures and quantities naturally lend themselves to emphasis and exaggeration, as in the parables of The Leaven and The Sower—than to explain why they have disappeared.

The 'Julicher' Reconstruction of the Story

Having understood, as far as one can, the processes whereby parables decay I am now in a position to attempt a reconstruction of the biblical parables. The first priority here is to understand the limits of the objective. As a reconstructionist I am not pretending that I can go behind the evangelists in terms of the content of the Gospels. I am only seeking to correct the picture the evangelists give of the parable-maker by the way in which they actually present the parables. In order to achieve a worthwhile reconstruction I do not have to be sure of the particular historical circumstances which called the parable forth. All I need to do is find a way of portraying the parable in question as a proper healing exercise. Never mind the minute chances of my ever getting this reconstruction 'spot-on'. At bottom, I am not concerned with what happened precisely at this long-lost event but only with seeing Jesus correctly.

In the first instance such a reconstruction involves cleaning up the story. Of course, if there are any real doubts about the possibility of achieving this, the project should be abandoned. However, this is rarely, if ever the case for the fact is that the very nature of parables demands for their stories an extremely high order of inner integrity.[24] I mean that in order to achieve their objects they have to be sharp and streamlined, with every component playing an integral part in making the overall thrust while offering no distractions. Because of this integrity and leanness, so long as the basic thrust is determinable, any additions or subtractions that have come about in the story through editorial work immediately hit one in the eye.

While the 'Julicher' reconstruction involves, in the main, teasing out the original story, it also implies detaching it from the surrounding material. This has to be done in order to judge it strictly on its own merits.[25] This is a sensitive issue, seeing that many scholars have forcibly argued that any attempt to get to the historical Jesus around the back of the evangelists is doomed to failure.

As a rule I agree with this principle. It is arrogant to pretend that one is better placed to judge what took place than those closest to the events. It is only in certain technical matters that we can claim to have the advantage, for example in our understanding of the mechanism of the parable speech-form or of the general historical process. However, in the parables of Jesus as they are presented in the Gospels, we are often faced with a stark and unusual choice: to follow the evangelists and interpret Jesus' stories against their basic integrity or to cut ourselves loose from the evangelists' interpretations and dare to follow the central logic of the stories.[26]

24. 'The parables of Jesus have an organic unity and coherence. They come down through retelling protected by their shape and hardness like quartz nuggets in a stream.' Wilder, *Language*, p. 90.

25. '...the issue is imagining the parable outside the Gospel narrator's point of view, imagining the parable not as imagined by the Gospel narrator but with the parable's implied speaker as narrator.' Scott, *Hear Then*, p. 68.

26. Dodd, *Kingdom*, p. 97.

In other words I believe that because parables, alone among speech-forms, *contain in their phenomenal natural integrity and sparseness an inbuilt resistance to editorial manipulation*, we are presented with a quite unique opportunity to do what is generally impossible: to go behind the evangelists and encounter to a degree the way in which the historical Jesus actually operated.

Stripping away the surrounding material from the parables does not mean casting doubts on its genuineness or consigning the evangelists' interpretations to oblivion. Indeed, the excised material may appear perfectly authentic in its own right. Likewise, once the story has been allowed to speak for itself the setting which the evangelist has provided may appear perfectly adequate, in which case there is no obligation to pursue the matter further.[27]

However, the first principle must always be that the evangelists' interpretations have to justify themselves. Not only because it is most improbable that they received the parables in such a state that they could be nearly certain about them, but also because in the final analysis *every* interpretation of a parable must be vindicated by its story's own 'logic'.

The 'Dodd' Reconstruction of the Background

While it takes a skilled writer to describe adequately the incident which gave rise to a parable, it is a more straightforward exercise than explaining its background since the former can be achieved by a simple narration of events whereas explaining the background demands an analytic style. For example, most people can make an attempt at giving an account of something which has recently happened but few possess the analytic skills needed to explain its significance.

This, of course, was even truer of the biblical writers. David's biographer would have been incapable of offering the sort of background sketch that Peter Niesewand gave for the parable of the donkey. He simply did not possess the necessary analytical tools. Fortunately he was not obliged to, since his own work was placed in the context of other writings which set out at length the stories of the kingship controversies. We should not be surprised, therefore, that the evangelists' attempts at reconstructing backgrounds are rather crude.

But this was not their only problem. The sheer number of stories they were dealing with made it impossible for them to attempt to reconstruct

27. For example, 'The Place for a Doctor' (Pb. 1).

more than a few. They therefore adopted two general approaches. Either they used parable stories in pairs or even triplets, or else they knitted a number of them together with other types of logia to form extended discourses. One can understand that, from their point of view, such solutions must have appeared extremely neat. However, for modern readers, both approaches were quite disastrous since they undermined the parables' essential functions.

In practice, using parables in pairs is self-defeating. No two illustrations make exactly the same impact, so the terms of one inevitably confuse or deform the terms of the other.[28] Furthermore telling parables in pairs is psychologically disastrous. Parable-makers only get one bite at the cherry. If they do not make a success of it the safest course of action is to withdraw!

One presumes the evangelists knew that Jesus had occasionally spoken at length to audiences. However, there would have been no record of what was actually said. So they would naturally have seized on these all too numerous isolated parable stories as a body of material on which to build their accounts of such discourses.

However, even if critical examination had not made it patently evident that these sermons are a contrivance it should be obvious that an extended monologue is not a suitable setting for parables. For, as I have already insisted, parables are not descriptive illustrations that one can use simply to elucidate points. They are, on the contrary, 'conversation stoppers' which fix their light compellingly on specific problems which have been raised, to the exclusion of everything else, so their presence within a sermon would have been highly disruptive and appeared most odd.

This being the case, if there is to be any hope of reconstructing the parables' backgrounds, the stories must be abstracted from their present contexts and, by virtue of the reader concentrating solely on their basic 'logic', judged for their usefulness as instruments of healing in the kinds of situations the evangelists tell us Jesus was involved in. If this fails we may even be forced to rely on our own experience of the general run of twisted attitudes that one encounters in any human society: people paralysed by guilt, consumed by greed, or who try to justify being rich when others are poor.

---

28. You can see this actually happening when commentators transfer aspects of one 'twin' parable to another, without any warrant in terms of the logics of the stories. See p. 136 below.

The Incident Reconstruction

When it comes to reconstructing incidents we find ourselves in uncharted waters so we have to consider carefully what is involved. An incident consists of a number of unique decisions, actions and occurrences; it is the overall way in which these fit together that determines the nature of the incident in question. In other words, the character of an incident lies in its detail; the more detail you possess the greater your appreciation of it.

Now because these details are unique their loss is clearly irreparable. There is no way we can pretend to deduce them from the story or background. Once gone they are beyond recall. This makes the reconstruction of an incident quite different from the reconstruction of a background. Whereas there are times when we can be fairly confident that we have recovered the correct background of an isolated parable story we can never hope to recreate the exact incident that caused it to be delivered.

It is natural therefore to wonder if a reconstruction of the incident is possible. However, there are two reasons why I do not despair. First, although it is true that an incident consists of an assemblage of unique details, I see it as falling within a general category of similar incidents. For example, the evangelists indicate a number of occasions when Jesus was criticized for going around with the wrong sort of people and again another set of occasions in which he was accused of showing disrespect for the customs and traditions of his people. Thus, although it is true that I can never hope to recover the lost incidents themselves it is quite conceivable that I may be able to determine the general category into which each falls.

For a case in point, Luke does not have any doubt that The Lost Sheep (Pb. 26), The Lost Coin (Pb. 52) and The Prodigal Son (Pb. 53) were answers to people who accused Jesus of consorting with publicans and sinners:

> Now the tax-collectors and sinners were all drawing near to hear him.
> And the Pharisees and the scribes murmured, saying, 'This man receives sinners and eats with them.' So he told them this parable... (15.1-3)

However, I believe I can go further still and place into separate sub-categories each of the lost incidents that lie behind these parables. First, because of the economic aspect of the lost sheep story (a shepherd's sheep being his livelihood), I suggest the criticism made by some unknown person on this occasion was that it was not 'economic' for Jesus to waste his time with people who had got themselves into unnecessary scrapes; that to be effective he should concentrate on those who kept their heads down and obeyed the Law.

Secondly, because of the way the story of the lost coin dwells on a woman's obsessive absorption with the loss of something relatively trivial I suggest the accusation against Jesus was that his attitude towards social dropouts was altogether excessive; that, in the first place, he allowed himself to be far too worried about their situations and then far too pleased by their pitiful responses to his attempts to help.

Thirdly, because of the way in which the story of the return of the prodigal culminates in the elder son's refusal to join the celebrations for his brother's return, I suggest the criticism voiced in this case was that in befriending criminals Jesus was being soft and forgetting the shocking things they had done.

This said, people will quite rightly claim that such categorizations are a poor substitute for a proper incident, which brings me to my second hopeful consideration. The reason I insisted it was necessary to reconstruct the incident was that this is the only way of experiencing the parable mechanism at work and therefore of appreciating its attitude-straightening impact. However, as long as we achieve an interpretation that includes this aspect, a recovery of the specific incident and therefore the precise attitude in question is not crucial. In fact, I see no reason not to invent suitable incidents for ourselves as substitutes for the lost ones, so long as we remain clear in our minds what we are doing and do not mislead anyone else.

You may feel that, given a scientific approach, a reconstruction that depends on imagining incidents is hardly proper. But this is to forget that imagination (in this context, 'hermeneutics') is necessary in all understanding, since the observer of any incident, especially those involving other human beings, can never be in possession of all the relevant facts, so some intelligent guesswork is necessary if any conclusion is to be arrived at. The art of hermeneutics at this level is both to know how to make your guesses as good as possible (since not all interpretations can be equally valid), and also to be aware of their limitations since there are many aspects of a forgotten incident which simply cannot be guessed.

So we have to ask ourselves: What are the criteria for a valid reconstruction in any given instance? The problem with understanding any

human behaviour is the hermeneutical distance between the predicaments of others and our own. The question thus becomes how we can
minimize this distance. Thinking about Jesus and his work it seems
inevitable that certain people will find themselves better placed to make
valid interpretive reconstructions of the lost incidents of his parables than
others. For example, I suggest that the poor and dispossessed are better
placed than the comfortably-off simply because Jesus' good news
specifically addressed their predicaments and so gave them priority. 'He
has anointed me to preach good news to the poor' (Lk. 4.18).

So whereas the *'Dodd' reconstruction*, aided as it is by a knowledge
of the situation pertaining in first-century Palestine, gives a clear advantage to the scholar over the person in the street, the *incident reconstruction* favours a category of people from which he or she is usually
excluded. This is not to infer that the modern scholar is well paid or lives
in an ivory tower. It is to take into account the status derived from
working in a university or parallel establishment. To be poor means,
among other things, to exist 'uneducated', without status: to pass
unrecognised in some menial job and to live forgotten in some urban
wilderness.

The Consequence Reconstruction

There are only five parables in the synoptic tradition in which the evangelists have recorded any consequences. Two of them, The Children and
the Pet Dogs (Pb. 11) and Two Debtors (Pb. 43), are rather exceptional;
the first in that Jesus, to his astonishment, discovered that his interlocutor was in no need of any enlightening; and the second because,
although an account is given of a conversation following on the delivery
of the parable, it reveals nothing of Jesus' opponent's reaction.

So there are only three cases in which we learn anything about how
people responded to Jesus' parables. When he tells the story of The
Servant of Two Masters (Pb. 18), Luke writes:

> The Pharisees, who were lovers of money, heard all this, and they
> scoffed at him. (16.14)

Where Jesus tells the rulers of the synagogue the story of The Rescued
Ox (Pb. 23), Luke comments:

> As he said this, all his adversaries were put to shame; and all the people
> rejoiced at all the glorious things that were done by him. (13.17)

Likewise where Mark records how Jesus told the temple authorities the parable of The Rebellious Tenants (Pb. 13) he adds:

> And they tried to arrest him, but feared the multitude, for they perceived that he had told the parable against them; so they left him and they went away. (12.12)

Because these consequences appear conventionalized, as if they had been simply deduced by the evangelists from general ideas of Jesus, a whole debate has opened up as to whether one should infer that Jesus was crucified at least in part because of his parable-making. For example, Crossan argues that Jesus 'was not crucified for parables but for the way of acting which resulted from the experience of God presented in the parables'.[29] However, against this particular view one has to insist that Jesus' speaking in parables, like his other healings, was in itself one of his significant modes of acting and not merely some sort of inspirational spur.

More recently, E.P.Sanders has claimed there is no warrant at all for the notion that Jesus was crucified because of his parables, maintaining that the only specific historical reasons that can be identified for his being put to death were his attack on the Temple and his message to sinners, both of which challenged the adequacy of the Law[30]

I venture to disagree. It is doubtful enough whether Jesus wished to modify the Law itself (Mt. 5.17, 18); but there is no real evidence that he was put to death because he espoused some particular burning issue. From the superscription on the cross it would seem that the Romans wanted people to believe that they were executing him because he constituted a political threat whereas the Sanhedrin ostensibly convicted him of blasphemy. But these were surely just pretexts.

In my view, the great weight of Christian tradition, 'orthodoxy' as one might call it, has always taught that the crucifixion can only be understood by seeing what Jesus did in terms of who he was (understood theologically) and vice versa. Christians have always felt that they knew perfectly well why Jesus was crucified. Because he was who he was, and acted as such, he inevitably revealed to people who came into contact with him their true nature. For the leaders of the community his presence quickly became unbearable. He removed their masks, exposing their alienating influence in such a way that, in spite of

---

29. Crossan, *In Parables*, p. 32.
30. E.P. Sanders, *Jesus and Judaism* (London: SCM Press, 1985), p. 293.

themselves, they became horribly aware that their cherished authority was pitted against God's. Is it surprising that their hearts were hardened and that they determined to destroy him? Since parable-making, like healing, was for Jesus a vital mode of action, and therefore of his being, it is certain that his use of parables contributed significantly to the decision to be rid of him.

Given that the reactions of most of Jesus' interlocutors are past recall, what would a reconstruction of the consequences of the parables involve? Certainly an attitude-changing parable would have inflicted pain on those at whom it was directed. So its consequences would have been either that its victim departed harbouring a serious grudge against Jesus or else experienced an agonizing change of mind—repentance—the healing offered by Jesus. It is important to keep this aspect in mind when interpreting parables, since if you ignore it you will almost inevitably find yourself thinking of them simply as teaching devices and interpret them accordingly. This is why I have insisted that we should see the parable phenomenon as including everything from background through to consequences.

Most errors in understanding the parables of the New Testament arise as a consequence of an avoidance of the demolition/reconstruction task. Indeed the evangelists' misleading allegorizations were themselves the result of an inability to properly reconstruct the stories. Before modern scholarship there was, of course, never any question of doubting the evangelists' work. However, the fact that people subsequently needed to invent further allegorizations was a disguised admission of the fact that the evangelists' work left something to be desired.

Because the Gospels' naive reconstructions or loosely strung-together, parable-filled, sermons sound increasingly crude to modern ears, Christians are defensively apt to paper over the cracks. Apologists try to deny the evidence, making out that if you take the trouble to study the text properly (that is, to bring to bear upon it a considerable ingenuity) you find, or at least can make it appear, that the evangelists' work makes perfectly good sense.

Such a refusal to admit the obvious flaws and incongruities in the way in which the synoptic writers present their material is systematic among fundamentalists, but it is a brave Christian who can claim to be entirely free of it.[31] Both Dodd and Jeremias tend to turn a blind eye when an

31. Drury escapes the problem by making a positive feature of such flaws and incongruities. *Parables*, pp. 44-48, 58-59, 64.

evangelist's interpretation distorts, in some slight way, the actual parable story. They follow slavishly the evangelists' interpretations except where these are very far-fetched or contradictory, as in the saying about salt (Pb. 12). It is only in these few instances, when happily freed from the evangelists' influence, that they show they are capable of taking the logic of the story seriously. So it appears that even the errors of reconstructionists are mainly due to their failure to carry through their project.

Again, the new hermeneuticists' decision to abandon the search for what the parables meant to their first-century hearers and their pretence that Jesus' stories can be understood as disembodied 'works of art' are really just a sophisticated way of covering-up the painful awareness that the parables as they stand cry out for a serious, far-reaching remedy. Instead of risking the dangers of a full demolition/reconstruction job, they have preferred the easier way of imposing on the stories a new set of general meanings, just as Julicher had done before them.

When it comes to scholars like Blomberg and Drury, who continue to insist against the evidence upon an allegorical interpretation of the parables, the problem seems to be that they simply cannot bring themselves to admit either that to some extent the evangelists 'got it wrong' or that their getting it wrong matters. In their case, as in others, there seems to be something of a wilful blindness to the need for reconstruction.

Chapter 6

PARABLE-MAKING

Jesus as Parable-Maker

In this book I have examined the different models that have been proposed at various times for understanding what Jesus was about when he
spoke in parables:

1. The *coded message* model with its belief that Jesus did not
    want certain people to understand what he was saying.
2. The *general illustration* model in which Jesus is seen as using
    picturesque stories to teach high notions of morality to simple
    countryfolk.
3. The *riddle* model in which Jesus is envisaged as arresting people
    with strange stories and teasing their minds into active thought.
4. The various *creative art* models in which Jesus is seen as shar-
    ing his own religious awareness by means of 'poetic' or
    'musical' performances.
5. The conservatives' *concealment* model in which Jesus is pic-
    tured as revealing his message only gradually so as to give
    people the necessary space in which to make their own
    commitments.

Everyone who puts forward a model is, essentially, attempting to give
a consistent rationale of what Jesus was doing when he spoke in parables. In this sense all the above attempts are successful. But if a model is
to convince it must fulfil two further criteria. First, it has to show that
the parabolic mechanism is capable of delivering what the model asks of
it and, secondly, it has to present a picture of Jesus which conforms with
that portrayed by the rest of the synoptic material. The 'riddle' and
'concealment' models are, in my view, unable to meet the first criterion;
and the 'coded message', 'general illustration' and 'creative art' models
fail the second.

Over against these unsatisfactory models I have attempted to establish my own alternative in which parables are understood as designed, in the main, to deal with people's twisted attitudes. Accordingly, Jesus' parable-making is to be seen as part and parcel of his ministry of *healing*. I pointed out that Jeremias came close to envisaging this healing model when he described the parables as 'weapons of controversy'.[1] What might be described as a 'merciless' targeting of people's sick attitudes is a prerequisite of their restoration to health; only by means of such an exposure are they given any real chance to repent. But I explained that Jeremias never made the link between parables and miracles and had no concern to establish a model since his embrace of the 'hold-all' theory meant an abandonment of the search for a single form.

I argued that this healing model satisfied the first of the above criteria when in Chapters 2 and 4 I analysed the working of the parable mechanism in contrast to the other two-dimensional speech forms. I showed how the parable produces a *concentrated illumination* of its subject matter, thereby forcing on the hearer a certain awareness: it being the acceptance of this awareness by people with a deformed attitude that brings them healing. So, all that remains is to demonstrate that this same healing model presents a picture of Jesus which squares with the non-parabolic material in the Gospels.

This is not hard to do. We know from the synoptic tradition that Jesus was concerned to prepare people for 'the coming of the Kingdom'. If this involved him in healing minds and bodies, all the more would it involve him in healing attitudes. Indeed most of the non-parabolic logia in the synoptic Gospels, as for example in the Sermon on the Mount, are directed to people's attitudes; and so to see the parables as similarly directed makes them all of a piece with the rest of the tradition. Therefore, in terms of the two criteria above the healing model stands vindicated. But by explaining a number of technical characteristics that commentators on the Gospels over the years have noted about Jesus' parables, I would now like to demonstrate how this model recommends itself even more cogently. In doing so I do not want to work with one of Jesus' own parables for fear of giving the impression of penetrating his mind. So here is one from a friend of mine.

> A doctor one day received a visit in her surgery from a patient who was a chain-smoker. The man asked her for some medicine for his cough. The

1. Page 13 above.

doctor realized at once that the man's cough was not the result of an infection but of his smoking, so instead of prescribing medicine she told him this story.

> There was a man who lived by a lake and kept a boat for fishing. Over the years he failed to keep the boat in repair so water began to come in between the planks. At first he could bail it out well enough using a tea cup. However, the day came when the boat leaked so fast that the cup wouldn't do the trick. As the boat filled up with water he said to himself: 'Why the devil didn't I bring a saucepan!'[2]

It is clear from this example that when one uses the healing model the parable-maker is to be seen in the first place as *identifying a problem attitude*. Here the attitude exhibited by the chain-smoker actually presents itself when he walks through the surgery door and asks for medicine for his cough, so the doctor's parable is understood as a *riposte*. From the evangelists' attempts to sketch-in parabolic incidents in certain cases it would seem that they also saw Jesus' parables functioning most naturally as rejoinders. Indeed I have already drawn attention to this feature when noting that Jesus did not use parables as part of a studied presentation of an argument but employed them in the cut and thrust of 'market-place' debates.[3]

In the above example, the parable-maker identifies the problem attitude by realizing that her patient has a blockage, is curiously blind to something that is self-evident. The chain-smoker knows perfectly well that it is foolish to address symptoms which declare the presence of a fault while leaving the fault itself untreated. Like everyone else he has come across this *common experience* many times in his life and has no need to have it explained. It is not the common experience itself that he obtusely ignores but its relevance to his own situation. Indeed one might even say that the cause and effect relationship—between smoking and coughing—which he is unable to see because of the trap he is in, is in some sense also well known to him. He is holding himself prisoner.

The parable-maker uses her patient's perfect understanding of the need to treat the causes of faults rather than their symptoms by telling a story whose *thrust* spotlights this common experience and invites him to make the connection with his personal predicament. The thrust of the doctor's story is that the fisherman would have done well to concentrate

---

2.   This is a *doctor's* parable and is not for the use of those who are mainly concerned to be 'politically correct' about smoking.

3.   See pp. 64-65 above.

on mending his boat rather than on improving his bailing technique; but the doctor's purpose in telling the story is clearly to turn a searchlight on the chain-smoker's situation by presenting him with the common experience of treating causes rather than symptoms.

It would appear that Dodd was striving to isolate this central feature of parables, their concentrated thrust, when he took up Julicher's formula that parables only make one point. However his 'riddle' model could not (any more than the others) do justice to this principle, for there is no way in which a riddle can be said to 'point to' (illuminate) its solution. Nor is there anything about the nature of riddles that insists on one-point solutions.

It is true that, because of the damage inflicted upon Jesus' stories during the process of their transmission, their thrusts have in many cases been obscured. Yet, in spite of this, I have not found a single case in which real doubt remains as to what the thrust originally was. This is why I have dared to suggest that we should cut ourselves free of the evangelists' interpretive apron strings and follow where the stories themselves lead.[4]

Another connected feature of parables that has often been noticed but which preceding models have been unable to explain is the fact that a parable at its best is *lean and without embellishment*. Thus Dodd and Jeremias:

> If the parable is drawn out to any length, it is likely that details will be inserted which are suggested by their special appropriateness to the application... But in the true parable any such details will be kept strictly subordinate to the dramatic realism of the story, and will not disturb its unity.[5]

> ...comparison of the parallel forms in which the parables have come down to us shows the correctness of the view that in many cases parables have undergone elaboration, and that the simpler version represents the original.[6]

However, when one adopts the healing model it becomes perfectly obvious why an expert parable-maker eschews all decorations since any

---

4. This does not mean that we take the liberty to go beyond the general witness of the tradition. It simply means that we dare to set aside the evangelists' specific reconstructions.

5. Dodd, *Kingdom*, p. 20.

6. Jeremias, *Parables*, pp. 30-31.

unnecessary element in the story would tend to divert attention from its basic logic, the very generator of the healing process.

There is another typical feature of the parables that has often been noticed but which no model has so far been able to explain satisfactorily, and that is their lack of moralization. One tends to notice this aspect in a rather roundabout fashion: the way in which commentators (including in the first place the evangelists) tend to undermine the inherent strength of the parables by moralizing them. Under the heading 'The Hortatory Use of Parables by the Church', Jeremias shows how the evangelists thus altered the original stories. But, as Crossan points out, he did so basically to excuse what they did:

> It would seem that allegorization has received a much worse reception in recent scholarship than has moralization... In the classic work by J. Jeremias on the parables much less space and a far kinder judgment is accorded to the tradition's moralizing than to its allegorizing...: 'by the hortatory application the parable is not misinterpreted but "actualized".'... So also in more recent studies on the parables the interpretation... is still very heavy with moral application and ethical implication even if of a more existential than classical bent.[7]

Crossan is right for it is quite as damaging to moralize the parables as it is to allegorize them. But although he perfectly identifies the problem, Crossan's musical adaptation of the 'creative art' model hardly shows why moralizings are out of place. It is only when you take up the healing model and learn to treat the story's logic as the central feature of the parabolic mechanism that it becomes obvious how this is undermined by any moral labelling of the characters in the story.

In the parable of The Rebellious Tenants, Thomas calls the owner of the vineyard 'good' and Matthew has the hearers describe the tenants as 'wretches'. However, by employing such epithets they simply demonstrate a lack of confidence in the story's logic which functions quite independently of the moral character of the landlord or the tenants.[8] Probably Thomas felt the need to shelter God from the odium of likening him to a hated foreigner but it was a clear mistake; instead of adding weight this moral opprobrium tends to obscure the story's thrust, which depends on the *inevitability* of the connection between the tenants' actions and their fate. Indeed it would have been safer to make the landlord a rogue and the tenants honest; the moral pressure would then

---

7.   Crossan, 'In Parables', pp 79-80.
8.   See p. 145 below.

have interfered less with the logic of the story since it would have been going in the opposite direction.

Once one sees this it becomes clear that giving moral labels to the characters in a parable's story is just a cheap way to achieve an imitation thrust. I say cheap since it is produced by merely adding a couple of adjectives to the story, whereas the genuine thrust is developed by the way in which the 'logic' unravels. Of course the reason why the evangelists resorted to such tactics was that they found themselves in the difficult position of reconstructing parables which had lost their applications (backgrounds, incidents and consequences). However, as soon as moral labels appear you can be certain that the person responsible for them has got it wrong. For this reason, it is very important to exclude them from the parables' titles, for example from The [Good] Samaritan.[9]

Another way of highlighting this same feature of parables is to point out that they appeal to hard, down-to-earth 'commonsense' and not to inferred 'truths', be these moral, aesthetic or religious. For example in the parables of the rabbis, as in those of Jesus, the thrust is often developed out of the sheer economic practicality of the situations described:

> ... a husbandman possessing two cows, one of which is strong and the other weak. Upon which does he place the yoke? Is it not upon her which is strong? Even so does the Holy one, blessed be He, try the righteous...[10]

This aspect of parables is so striking that commentators are all but obliged to note it in passing. Thus Dodd:

> They [parables] are the natural expression of a mind that sees truth in concrete pictures rather than conceives it in abstractions.[11]

However, because this is never taken into account in the parabolic model the very same commentators end up producing interpretations of the parables that are moralistic, sentimental or 'spiritual'. This danger is lessened if my healing model is used. Here the inherent power of the thrust is seen as all-important and the thrust can only be experienced as powerful if it is seen as appealing directly to common sense.

---

9.   B.B. Scott also notes this problem of titling. Explaining his decision to give all the parables neutral headings he writes: 'The parables originally had no titles, and the traditional titles frequently embed summaries of inherited meanings.' *Hear Then*, p. 4.

10.   Feldman, *Rabbis*, pp. 30-31.

11.   Dodd, *Kingdom*, p. 16.

Yet another feature of parables, often remarked on, is that instead of lecturing about what is right and true they present a comparison and simply invite people to draw their own conclusions:

> ...the parable has the character of an argument, in that it entices the hearer to a judgement upon the situation depicted, and then challenges him, directly or by implication, to apply that judgement to the matter in hand.[12]

As Dodd also remarks elsewhere in his book,[13] parables properly close with a question. Perhaps he identifies the characteristic so unerringly because it happens to square with his idea that parables are riddles. However, it fits equally well with the healing model as long as it is made perfectly clear that what one is talking about is the sort of healings one finds in the synoptic Gospels, in which the patient actively cooperates. A parable should come in the form of a question because it is not only the exposure of a sick attitude but also the offer of a correction. This is why I make a habit of presenting my understanding of a parable's analogy in an interrogatory form.[14]

One final comment on the justification of the healing model. I believe that the use of the general illustration, riddle and concealment models all too easily leads to an unwarranted intellectualization of the parables; they are described as 'making points' and 'conveying meaning'. As I see it, only the creative art models of the new hermeneutic show a concern to make room for people to see that with parables something more than just the mind is involved. However, in doing so they tend to take the user too far the other way. By concentrating on what they see as a parable's aesthetic, existential or spiritual aspects they undermine the sharpness and precision of its attack, making its impact diffuse. This is not true of the healing model. Here, room is made for a parable's intellectual and non-intellectual aspects without introducing any vagueness.[15]

Parable-Making Today

Crossan has argued against Jeremias that parables are of no use when directed to avowed opponents:

12. Dodd, *Kingdom*, p. 21. See also the contention of the new hermeneutic that parables are open-ended, p. 43 n. 13 above.

13. Dodd, *Kingdom*, p. 94.

14. See Part II of this book.

15. A friend of mine from Glasgow has a much better description of this intrinsic flaw in the new hermeneutic approach. He calls it 'arty-farty'. However, I could not quite bring myself to include such an expression in the main body of my text!

Parables and analogies are notoriously weak in converting or convincing those who are not open to their vision or are clearly opposed to their purpose, but they are just as notoriously persuasive for those who are at least open to their challenge.[16]

This statement warrants close attention because, although inaccurate, it contains just enough truth to make it ring a bell for us. If it were accurate we would have to see parables as aimed at initiates or at least people who had shown an interest in Jesus' teaching. However, such an understanding conflicts not only with Mark's statement that they were devised expressly for outsiders, and with the 'Isaiah' logion that they were designed to harden opposition, but also with the memory of the early church. In the great majority of cases where the parabolic incident has been recorded the opponent is shown as critical of Jesus.

Crossan gives his game away when he cites Ezra Pound as saying that 'You can prove nothing by analogy'.[17] The mistake is in postulating parables as frontal attacks that convince by the sheer weight of their argument. Taken as such they are certainly unconvincing. But, of course, parables are not frontal attacks. They are flanking movements designed to explode under peoples' guard and make them aware despite themselves. As such they can be most effective, as Nathan showed.

It is true that the reaction to any parable will almost certainly depend on the person's relationship with the parable-maker. David, you will remember, repented—although one imagines it was touch and go. If the Isaiah quotation in Mark 4.12 was used by Jesus in connection with his habit of speaking in parables (as I am inclined to believe) it would seem that he did not use parables foolishly believing that he was likely to convert his enemies. He told his stories to 'get under their skin': 'that seeing they should indeed see and not perceive'. And this he most emphatically succeeded in doing for, as I believe, it was because he successfully unmasked the attitudes of those in authority that they found him unbearable and therefore determined to be rid of him.

Since parables can be such a powerful way of getting at twisted attitudes should we set about using them ourselves? It is only in asking this question that one begins to see the element of truth in Crossan's assertion cited above. The fact is that parable-making was the product of a pre-scientific culture, which explains why parable-making persists in

16. Crossan, *In Parables*, pp. 74-75.
17. Crossan, *In Parables*, p. 75.

certain parts of the world, having disappeared almost completely from Western society.

In our current ideological debates we still sometimes use simile and metaphor to describe, denounce and exhort but it is almost unheard of to use parables to expose peoples' twisted attitudes. The fact is that we have what are considered to be better means of doing so. We tell people straight out what we think of their behaviour, using the full range of our knowledge of the various branches of sociological research.

Only very occasionally do people use parables, like this one told me by a friend:

> When I was a young curate we had in our church a number of worthy folk who found the boisterous behaviour of the adolescents during their club hour in the church hall unseemly and out of place. In one of our parochial church council meetings they began to tell me that I should either keep the youngsters in better discipline or else find some other place for them to meet. I replied by telling them this story:

> 'There was once a farmer who always became impatient during the long winters since he could do no work on his property. He would pace up and down looking out of the window, cursing the wind, the rain, the snow and the ice. However, on going out at the beginning of spring, what did he find but that the elements he had so maligned had done the work for him: killing off the pests and preparing the soil for ploughing.'

However even if, as here, parables are well constructed, their use tends to make the parable-maker sound slightly quaint. That said, I have known a person who could get away with it. He was a self-educated manual worker who had become a staff member on one of the teams of the French Protestant Industrial Mission. During our annual get-togethers he would remain for a long time listening intently but without participating. Then towards the end of the meeting he would rouse himself, explaining that he found it difficult to contribute to our theoretical discussion but that the subject made him think of a parable. He would then proceed to tell us a story which would not only show that he was well aware of everything we had said but would often completely change the tenor of our debate.

We found it natural for him to use parables because that was actually how he thought problems through. We recognized the authenticity of his stories for it shone through everything he said. Most of us, however, do not share his culture so we find ourselves obliged to use more conventional methods of communication.

Fortunately, the attitude-straightening approach is by no means limited to story-telling. In fact parables are just one particular brand of straight talking, which reminds me of an incident in which I myself was involved. I had been moved by the Industrial Mission to Paris with another pastor and his wife and their five children. I was provided with a single room in which there was a sink to wash in but to take a bath I was obliged to do so in their flat.

On my first visit I found the bathroom liberally furnished with towels but having been brought up with middle-class principles I did not feel I could use any of them for fear of being accused of taking one belonging to someone else. So I went in some embarrassment to ask the pastor's wife if she could possibly, on this occasion, provide me with a towel, as I had not brought one with me. She looked up from what she was doing in some surprise and with eyebrows raised replied, 'Why, do you find there are not sufficient towels already in the bathroom?' Mortified, I muttered something incoherent and went to run my bath. But her words had struck home and I was cured. Since that day I have never treated bath towels as private property!

So it is perfectly possible to address twisted attitudes without resorting to illustrations. However, there is something about the use of the intrinsic similarity between fundamentally different situations that captures our attention and helps to open our eyes. Recently while struggling with the writing of this book I managed to work myself into such a state that I became ill and lost weight. At first nothing my doctor prescribed seemed to do me much good and though I tried to tell myself that I was being stupid I began to suspect that I might have a cancer. In this way I gave myself, quite unnecessarily, a bad few days.

Now, I work as a porter in a hospital and late one evening one of the doctors phoned to ask for help. She explained that there was something wrong with the door of her room in the Residence and she could not get in. When I arrived she told me she had had some trouble with the lock the previous evening but that now something must have broken because her key simply wouldn't turn at all. When she gave me the key I immediately understood the reason for this: by its number I could see that it belonged to a completely different room.

When she found the right key in her bag she apologized profusely for disturbing me and I—I must admit—was enjoying her embarrassment when suddenly it dawned that this was a 'parable' meant for me. Just as she had given us both unnecessary trouble and made herself look foolish by jumping to conclusions—diagnosing a fault in the lock simply because she had had a little difficulty with it the previous evening—so I was being equally foolish in persuading myself that I had cancer simply because I had lost a bit of weight.

It would seem that our capacity to recognize lateral, logic-based illustrative situations is not impaired, even though we are no longer in the habit of turning them into stories to tell one another. Our achievement of a certain linguistic sophistication means that something rather special has disappeared from our culture. Let us hope that this is only a temporary loss and that we will find new illustrative means of helping each other to see things to which we have allowed ourselves to become blind.

CATEGORIZATION OF SPEECH-FORMS IN THE SYNOPTIC TRADITION

One-Dimensional Forms

Models		Mk	Mt.	Lk.	Thom.
1.	Jesus as Receiver of a Child	9.36	(18.5)	9.48	
2.	Receiving the Kingdom Like a Child	10.15	18.14	18.17	22
3.	The Widow who Gives a Mite	12.43		21.3	

Paradoxes					
1.	The First Last	9.35			
2.	Having/Given More; Having not/ Taken away	4.25	13.12 25.29	8.18	
3.	Saving Life/Losing it; Losing Life/ Finding it	8.35	10.39 16.25	9.24	

Two-Dimensional Forms

Representations:

Figures		Mk	Mt.	Lk.	Thom.
1.	Things Said in the Dark	4.22	10.26	12.3	(6)
2.	Leaven of the Pharisees	8.15	16.6	12.1	
3.	Tasting Death	9.1			1 (et al.)
4.	Salted with Fire	9.49			
5.	Drinking the Cup	10.38	20.22		
6.	Devouring Widows' Houses	12.40		20.47	
7.	Removing the Cup	14.36	26.39	22.42	
8.	Bringing a Sword		10.34	(12.51)	16
9.	Locking the Door of the Kingdom		23.13		
10.	Your House is Forsaken		23.38	13.35	
11.	Receiving without Paying		10. 8		
12.	The Easy Yolk		11.29		
13.	The Uprooted Plant		15.13		40
14.	Lost Sheep of the House of Israel		15.24		

	Mk	Mt.	Lk.	Thom.
15. The Keys of the Kingdom		16.19		
16. Key of Knowledge			11.52	39a
17. A Baptism to be Baptised with			12.50	

Acted Figures

	Mk	Mt.	Lk.	Thom.
1. Eating Bread	14.22	26.26	22.19	
2. Drinking Wine	14.23	26.27	22.20	

Mythical Imagery

	Mk	Mt.	Lk.	Thom.
1. The Worm that Does Not Die	9.48			
2. Unclean Spirit		12.43	11.24	
3. One Taken Another Left		24.40	17.34	61
4. The Last Judgment Scene		25.34		
5. Satan Falling from Heaven			10.18	

Instances:

Examples   None

Illustrations:

Similes   Simple

	Mk	Mt.	Lk.	Thom.
1. Sheep without a Shepherd		6.34	9.36	
2. Sheep among Wolves		10.16a	10. 3	
3. Serpents and Doves		10.16b		39b
4. Jonah in the Whale		12.40	11.30	
5. The Grain of Mustard Seed		17.20	17. 6	
6. Whitewashed Tombs		23.27		
7. The Hen and her Brood		23.37	13.34	
8. Lightning		24.27	17.24	
9. The Day of Noah / Lot		24.37	17.26	
10. Righteous Shine like the Sun		13.43		
11. The Snare			21.34	
12. Sifted like Wheat			22.31	
13. Graves Not Seen			11.44	

Dissimilar

	Mk	Mt.	Lk.	Thom.
14. Foxes and their Holes / Birds and Nests		8.20	9.58	86
15. Red Sky at Night / A Cloud in the West		16. 2	12.54	

More-than

		Mk	Mt.	Lk.	Thom.
16.	The Birds of the Air / Ravens		6.26	12.24	36
17.	The Lilies of the Field		6.28	12.27	
18.	The Grass in the Field		6.30	12.28	
19.	Sparrows for a Penny		10.29	12. 6	
20.	The Queen of the South		12.42		

Modified More-than

		Mk	Mt.	Lk.	Thom.
21.	The Camel and the Needle's Eye	10.25	19.24	18.25	
22.	The Master Called Beelzebub		10.25		

Metaphors

		Mk	Mt.	Lk.	Thom.
1.	Fishers of Men	1.17	4.19	5.10	
2.	The Eye that Causes you to Sin	9.43	5.29/ 18.8		
3.	Life as a Ransom	10.45			
4.	A Den of Thieves	11.17	21.13	19.46	
5.	Mote and Beam		7.3	6.41	26
6.	The Dead Burying their Dead		8.22	9.60	
7.	Harvest and Labourers		9.37	10. 2	73
8.	The Disciple and his Cross		10.38	14.27	55
9.	Revealed to Babes		11.25	10.21	
10.	Salt of the Earth		5.13		
11.	Light of the World		5.14		
12.	Sounding a Trumpet		6. 2		
13.	Left Hand / Right Hand		6. 3		62
14.	Wolves in Sheep's Clothing		7.15		
15.	Brood of Vipers		12.34/ 23.33		
16.	Peter the Rock		16.18		
17.	Straining out a Gnat		23.24		
18.	Little Flock			12.32	
19.	Purses that Do Not Grow Old			12.33	

Parables

		Mk	Mt.	Lk.	Thom.
1.	The Place for a Doctor	2.17	9.12	5.31	
2.	The Wedding Guests	2.19	9.15	5.34	104
3.	The Patch on the Garment	2.21	9.16	5.36	47d
4.	New Wine in Old Wineskins	2.22	9.17	5.37	47c
5.	The Divided Kingdom	3.24	12.25	11.17	
6.	The Strong Man's House	3.27	12.29	11.21	35
7.	The Sower	4. 3	13. 3	8.5	9

		Mk	Mt.	Lk.	Thom.
8.	The Lamp	4.21	5.15	8.16/	33
				11.33	
9.	The Growing Seed	4.26			(21c)
10.	The Mustard Seed	4.31	13.31	13.19	20
11.	The Children and the Pet Dogs	7.27	15.26		
12.	Salt	9.50	5.13	14.34	
13.	The Rebellious Tenants	12.1	21.33	20.9	65
14.	The Budding Fig tree	13.28	24.32	21.29	
15.	The Night Porter	13.34		12.36	
16.	The Litigant		5.25	12.58	
17.	The Eye		6.22	11.34	(24)
18.	The Servant of Two Masters		6.24	16.13	47a
19.	Looking for Fruit		7.16	6.44	45a
20.	Judging Fruit Trees		7.17/	6.43	43
			12.33		
21.	Two House Builders		7.24	6.48	
22.	Children in the Market Place		11.16	7.32	
23.	The Rescued Ox		12.11	13.15/	
				14.5	
24.	Leaven		13.33	13.21	96
25.	Blind Guides		15.14	6.39	34
26.	The Lost Sheep		18.12	15.4	107
27.	The Banquet		22.2	14.16	64
28.	The Body and the Vultures		24.28	17.37	
29.	Waiting for the Burglar		24.43	12.39	21b/103
30.	The Servant Left in Charge		24.45	12.42	
31.	The Master's Capital		25.14	19.12	(41)
32.	The Town on a Hill		5.14		32
33.	Weeds among the Wheat		13.24		57
34.	Buried Treasure		13.44		109
35.	The Pearl		13.45		76
36.	The Drag-Net		13.47		8
37.	The Unforgiving Servant		18.23		
38.	The Labourers' Wages		20.1		
39.	Two Sons		21.28		
40.	The Torch-Bearers		25.1		(75)
41.	Sheep and Goats		25.32		
42.	New and Old Wine			5.39	47b
43.	Two Debtors			7.41	
44.	The Samaritan			10.30	
45.	The Insistent Neighbour			11.5	
46.	The Rich Farmer			12.16	63/(72)
47.	The Barren Fig Tree			13.6	
48.	The Locked Door			13.25	

	Mk	Mt.	Lk.	Thom.
49. Precedence at Table			14.8	
50. The Tower Builder			14.28	
51. A King Going to War			14.31	
52. The Lost Coin			15.8	
53. The Prodigal Son			15.11	
54. The Indestructible Steward			16.1	
55. The Rich Man and Lazarus			16.19	
56. The Master and his Servant			17.7	
57. The Widow and the Judge			18.2	
58. Two Men in the Temple			18.10	
59. Children in the Field				21a
60. Children and their Garments				37
61. The Woman and the Broken Jar				97
62. The Assassin				98

More than Parables

	Mk	Mt.	Lk.	Thom.
63. A Father's Gift		7.9, 10	11.11, 12	

Compacted Parables

	Mk	Mt.	Lk.	Thom.
64. The Narrow Door		7.13	13.24	
65. Treasure from the Storehouse		12.35	6.45	45b
66. The Ploughman who Looks Back			9.62	
67. The Kindled Fire			12.49	10

Proverbs

	Mk	Mt.	Lk.	Thom.
1. Physician Heal Thyself			4.23	
2. Wisdom Justified by her Children		11.19	7.35	
3. The Dog in the Manger				102

Intractables

	Mk	Mt.	Lk.	Thom.
1. Casting Holy Things to Dogs		7.6		93
2. New and Old Treasure from the Store		13.52		
3. The Unclean Cup and Plate		23.25		89

Part II

The following pages contain reconstructions of twelve synoptic parables which I have selected according to two criteria. Those in Chapter 7 illustrate particular considerations which I have raised in Part I, whereas those in Chapter 8 are especially challenging of my interpretive thesis. Since I have not the space to include studies of all the synoptic parables I am obliged to demonstrate that my method of interpretation can handle these stories as adequately as any Jesus told.

Recent scholarship, especially the new hermeneutic, has not for the most part interested itself in trying to recover the original parabolic stories nor in placing them in contexts which are true to their logic. Therefore I have unashamedly built my reconstructions on the foundations laid by C.H. Dodd and J. Jeremias who pioneered in this field.

At the end of each study I offer my version of the parabolic analogy. But, a word of warning: the last thing I wish is for people to treat these analogies too seriously; at the end of the day each one of us has to make his or her own offering in this department since it is the obvious way of checking how one has understood the parable in question. But it is natural to feel slightly embarrassed by what one produces and to want to tear it up and throw it away since it is Jesus's parables and not our analogies that we wish to be left with.

One further thing should be borne in mind. My intention has been to 'reconstruct' how Jesus might have used each logion. By this I intend no disapproval of what is in the Gospels. For example, I have nothing against a preacher opening out the parable of The Rebellious Tenants (Pb. 13) as it has been allegorized by the evangelists. All I would suggest is that such a preacher should make it clear that what he or she is doing is coming to terms with a faith statement of the early church and not with Jesus' original purpose in telling the story.

Chapter 7

PARABLES EXEMPLIFYING IMPORTANT PRINCIPLES
OF RECONSTRUCTION AND INTERPRETATION

Being True to the 'Logic'

The primary issue I have raised in this book is that if you want to understand the intentions of a parable-maker you must follow at all costs the
logic of his or her story. This is a consideration in the reconstruction of
every reported parable. However, one parable in particular in the
Gospels lends itself as an especially apt illustration of this point since at
first sight there appear to be a number of alternative ways of reading it.

Leaven (Pb. 24)
Jeremias calculated that the amount of flour used by the woman would
be enough to produce bread for over a hundred people.[1] I am immediately persuaded that this feature is editorial since it distracts attention
from what the story as a whole, its logic, is saying.

On which aspect of bread-making did Jesus intend his audience to
focus? There appear to be four choices:

1. *Relative quantities* (of leaven and dough). This is the aspect
    emphasized by both Jeremias and the evangelists, and—if they
    are right—it makes the saying a variant of the parable of The
    Mustard Seed (Pb. 10).
2. *Partnership* (human with nature). As in the parable of The
    Growing Seed (Pb. 9).
3. *The catalytic aspect* (of the working of the leaven). Its impor-
    tance not for what it is in itself but for what it enables the
    dough to become. This is Dodd's line of argument,[2] and if he is
    right the parable is a variant of that of The Salt (Pb. 12).

1. Jeremias, *Parables*, pp. 147-48.
2. Dodd, *Kingdom*, pp. 143-44.

4. *The 'magical' aspect* (of the transformation of the dough) as is suggested by the 'hiding' of the leaven within the dough.

We must carefully consider each line of thought, for everything depends on which is selected.

First, the idea of 'relative quantities'. Although it has strong backers, this alternative has to be ruled out on the ground that, for the onlooker, the natural comparison is not between the morsel of leaven and the quantity of flour, or even between the morsel of leaven and the risen dough, but between the unrisen and the risen dough, and while there is a certain contrast here it is hardly spectacular. This becomes especially clear on comparison with the parable of The Mustard Seed.

Next the 'partnership' idea. In the parable of The Growing Seed, because of the time it takes for a grain of wheat to germinate and grow to maturity, there is a natural emphasis in the story upon the period in which the human agent is inactive. However, even though the Near Eastern method of bread-making—in which a morsel of dough left over from the last baking is used for leavening—is somewhat slower than the European use of fast-acting yeast it still only takes a matter of hours (Jeremias: 'overnight'). So, although the process of bread-making could be used to highlight the idea of partnership, a proficient story-teller would hardly have employed it since it does not automatically give rise to such an association in people's minds.

What about the 'catalytic' aspect? The emphasis in the story on the fact that the whole dough had risen seems to suggest such an effect, and it is certainly possible to use the leaven analogy to illustrate it: Like salt, a small lump of leaven has little food value on its own but its effect on dough (like salt's effect on food) is dramatic. However, while the term 'catalytic effect' precisely defines the remarkable process whereby salt enhances the flavour of food, it is not the aspect which naturally attracts attention in the preparation of dough for baking. Again, the reason for this is the time-scale. For the catalytic effect to be highlighted it has to take place virtually instantaneously: The cook tastes the soup and finds it insipid, puts in a teaspoon of salt and at once the flavour floods out.

Finally, we have the 'magical' aspect. I think it is this feature of the way leaven works that most naturally strikes the observer. Try to imagine yourself present 'naively', like a little boy watching his mother making bread.[3] The child watches his mother mix a small lump of dough

---

3. In this situation I do not think a first-century Jewish child would have reacted

kept from the last baking into the mass of her new dough, then sees her leave it in some warm place covered with a cloth. Coming back with her in the morning, he sees her remove the cloth and reveal the transformation: As if by magic the whole has swollen to twice its former size. 'Mummy, look what's happened!'

Here, once again, it is the time factor that is crucial to the observer's appreciation of the common experience on which the story is built. Timing is, after all, the essence of the magician's art. While amateurs perform their tricks either too rapidly or too slowly, the expert magician draws an audience irresistibly to the climax of the trick without overdoing any aspect or losing the people's attention.

In the case of the leaven working in the dough, the process is slow enough not to allow the onlooker to see what is happening (especially if everything is covered with a cloth), yet fast enough for the 'trick' to work. This is what makes it natural to describe the leaven as being 'hidden' in the dough until—hey presto!—all is revealed. Wouldn't any mother, given an audience of small children, instinctively play up the magic of what has happened?

What sort of defective attitude was Jesus targeting? The matter under scrutiny clearly involved some kind of change. Jesus' insight seems to have been that the process bringing about this change was not subject to human understanding: At first nothing has happened, then you find something has—but how?

I believe that the parable of The Growing Seed was Jesus' response to some indication that the disciples wanted *control* over the kingdom; its impact being that they should learn to work as junior partners with life. However, I suggest that the target of the parable of The Leaven was the disciples' desire to *understand* the 'mechanics' of the kingdom and how it comes about, its impact being that, when it comes to the development of people and society, you can never fully understand what is taking place. You must always operate expecting to be surprised.

Analogy:	As there is something magical about the way leaven works in the dough	So, when we witness the transformations accomplished by the kingdom, are we ever able to say *how* they have come about?

very differently from a twentieth-century European one (see Jeremias, *Parables*, p. 148).

Parousia Allegorizations

The most consistent way in which we find the evangelists interfering with the logic of Jesus' parables, and so misleading people about the parable-maker's intentions, is by allegorizing the stories. But as many scholars, beginning with Julicher, have drawn attention to this matter I have not thought it necessary to choose a parable myself to illustrate the point. However, associated with the evangelists' allegorizations of the parable stories is their unwarranted introduction of changes in order to make references to the parousia. This point has been less well grasped so I have chosen a parable to illustrate it.

The Litigant (Pb. 16)

If the logion at the end of the parable—about 'paying the last penny'—is original, as Jeremias believes,[4] then what is being dealt with here is a case of debt. However, it has to be said that there is nothing in the story itself to indicate that this is the case. Of course one can understand the early Christians wanting to see the story in this light, since it would have made the sense of the parable suit their parousia theology. They liked to teach that since people knew perfectly well what sort of judgment would be given on the last day they would do well to change their ways now before it was too late.

Whatever is the case we are clearly presented here with a choice. Either one person is dragging another unwillingly to court because of the latter's refusal to pay a debt or two people are rushing willingly to settle a dispute over a business transaction in which the legal niceties are not clear.

One important thing to bear in mind when deciding which alternative fits best is that in cases of unpaid debt the court's verdict is a foregone conclusion. With disputes, on the other hand, it is uncertain right up to the last moment. In stories about debt the question is: 'Will I manage to stay out of court?' In stories about disputes it is: 'On whose side will the judge come down?'

For a number of reasons I believe Jesus' story cannot be about debt.

1. The debt aspect gives the parable an unwarranted moralistic stance.

4. Jeremias, *Parables*, pp. 43-44.

2. If Jesus had wanted his audience to understand that the case was specifically one of debt, he would have supplied this information at the outset, so as to avoid any confusion, and not tucked it away right at the end.

3. Jewish law did not imprison people for debt (Jeremias believes this indicates that the story was about a non-Jewish situation. However, I find this idea somewhat far-fetched, and there is no other evidence in the story to support his claim).

4. Telling the man to settle before reaching the court would be an odd thing to do, considering that no debtor would allow himself to be dragged to court if he were in a position to pay. A debtor's only hope is for more time.

5. Luke writes 'make an effort to settle with him (your accuser) on the way, *lest he drag you to the judge...*' This is a curious thing to say, for the story maintains you are already on your way to court! Matthew's version contains the same oddity. I believe the story originally ran: '...lest the judge hand you over to the officer...'; the passage '...lest he drag you to the judge...' being added later by the early church in order to make the parable conform with its debt theology.

6. The story as it stands lacks tension, since it is clear from the start that the case is going to court and, as it is one of debt, what the outcome will be.

This last point is very significant. Jesus was a fine storyteller and his parable would certainly not have lacked tension. If, as I explained earlier, the original story had been about debt it would have been natural to generate the necessary tension by emphasizing the avoidance of the court appearance and the story would have looked something like this:

> If you owe your neighbour a sum of money be sure to pay it off as quickly as you can, otherwise his patience will wear out and he will drag you before the magistrate and...

In the story as it appears in the Gospels, there is no trace of this 'will I manage to stay out of court?' tension, introduced by the cautionary words 'be sure to pay it off as quickly as you can' in my story above. It could be argued that the necessary tension was present in Jesus' original story, but was lost with the disappearance of various elements in the process of its constant retelling. However, this is unlikely to have been the case, since it would have been in the interests of the early church to retain anything that justified a debt interpretation.

Here is a dispute: you and your opponent are rushing off to seek arbitration because both of you are convinced that the other is in the wrong. This is why neither of you is reluctant to go; why neither of you sees the advisability of settling the matter between yourselves; and why both of you are blind to the obvious likelihood that one of you is going to end up in a very nasty predicament.

In most courtroom dramas both parties think justice is on their side, the only important question being: 'Which way will the judgment go?' This story is no different. You have an important dispute with your opponent and believe yourself to be in the right. You are eager to have the matter settled. This story has nothing to say about the justice of your case; all it does is remind you that *judgments are unpredictable and can go either way.*

What, then, is the attitude being targeted? The story makes it clear. We all know what it is like to be involved in a dispute where both parties are convinced they are right and neither is prepared to give way; and we all know how distressing such situations are. For the individuals concerned, one way out is to get an impartial authority to judge between them. The parable targets the natural desire to avoid the pain and effort required in resolving disputes. The common experience upon which it is based is the unpredictability of judgments, and the thrust is that rushing off to find someone to arbitrate is short-sighted, since things might turn out very badly for you.

In what circumstances might such a parable have been used? We know of an occasion when a man asked Jesus to judge between himself and his elder brother in the matter of an inheritance (Lk. 12.13-14). Jesus is said to have rebuked the man. Perhaps he did so by telling him this parable (although Luke writes that he chose another, The Rich Farmer (Pb. 46), designed to evoke the shock of a completely different awareness).

Whatever prompted Jesus to tell this parable, I cannot help thinking that people must, on many occasions, have wished he would arbitrate in their disputes. Was this his way of getting them to take responsibility for their relationships with others, rather than rely on someone like him to smooth things over for them?

Analogy	As the result of a court case is unpredictable and the judge may not find in your favour	So is it wise of you to ask me to judge between you? Wouldn't you do better to reach mutual agreement without my involvement?

Moralization

Another way in which the evangelists betray the logic of the story is by introducing moral judgments.

The Master's Capital (Pb. 31)

Jeremias provides an important piece of background information, explaining that, according to Jewish law the way to guard someone's money, without accepting liability in a case of theft, was to bury it. On the other hand, to treat it casually by merely tying it up in a cloth rendered you responsible for making good its loss.[5]

Most commentators follow the evangelists in seeing the master as having a natural right to expect a certain standard of conduct from his servants, so when this is not forthcoming the culprit is branded as wicked, each interpreter supplying the epithets he chooses.[6] However, Jesus' story was not about a person who failed to behave as he *ought*. It was about a servant who foolishly believed his job was safe so long as he kept the rules, regardless of whether he fulfilled the expectations of his employer. The evidence to support this can be found in the construction of the story itself.

Had Jesus meant to focus attention on the moral culpability of the third servant he would have made it clear that the master had instructed him to trade with the money left in his keeping and that the man had accepted the responsibility. Only in such circumstances could the listener be expected to condemn his subsequent inaction.

However, when we turn to the Gospels we find that in both versions the servant shows that he was clearly loth to have anything to do with his master's money. Furthermore, Matthew fails even to establish the master's precise expectations. Of course Jesus' hearers would rightly have inferred that this dedicated money-maker was concerned that his liquid capital should not rest idle while he was away, but only Luke states that he specifically told his servants to trade with it.

Whatever conclusion Jesus' hearers may have come to regarding the expectations of the master, they would certainly have got the impression that the third servant was satisfied he had fulfilled his moral obligation to

5.   Jeremias, *Parables*, p. 61 n. 51.

6.   For us, the word 'servant' designates a person employed in a domestic capacity. This makes the idea of his taking risks with his master's capital somewhat improbable. But the servants in this story are actually persons employed to run the owner's affairs; hence they should really be described as members of his staff.

take due care of what had been committed to his trust. His actions along with his speech to the master on the latter's return make this abundantly plain.

All attempts to malign the third servant's character (Matthew, by having him clapped into prison; Luke, by altering the story so that he hides the money carelessly in a napkin; the Gospel according to the Hebrews, by having him use the money for his own personal enjoyment;[7] Dodd by calling him a barren rascal,[8] and Jeremias by describing him as inexcusably irresponsible[9]) founder on the fact that when you set out the story moralistically people invariably end up feeling slightly sorry for the man.

It is easy to understand why the evangelists moralized the story. They took the master to be God, and for a person to neglect God's gifts automatically merited reproach.[10] So as soon as the early church allegorized the parable a moralistic approach became inevitable, even though it reduced the thrust of the story to something altogether lifeless and banal—a wrong committed, a punishment administered.

Because Dodd and Jeremias are reluctant to go against Matthew and Luke they too fall into the same trap. However, I believe we are obliged to follow the thrust of the story, trusting to our conviction that the person who made it knew what he was doing. Following the logic of the story we are forced to recognize that the third servant, poor man, never wanted his master's money in the first place; that he accepted it only because he had no choice in the matter; and that having done so he proceeded to behave with perfect propriety by burying it safely.

So, if this man is neither wicked nor irresponsible, why is his master on his return so angry with him? Is it not because of something in his attitude; an inability, or unwillingness to face reality, a kind of blindness to his situation resulting from fear? The man knows his boss is an

7.   Eusebius writes that the Gospel of the Hebrews told of three servants, one who devoured his master's substance with harlots and flute-girls, another who multiplied the talent by trading, and another who hid it. The one was made to be shut up in prison, the second accepted, and the third only rebuked. M.R. James, *The Apocryphal New Testament* (Oxford: Clarendon Press, 1974), p. 3.

8.   Dodd, *Kingdom*, p. 112.

9.   Jeremias, *Parables*, p. 61.

10.   I am not here accusing the evangelists of finding a correspondence between the master and God, for this is perfectly justified (see pp. 83-84 above), nor of allegorizing the parable (as was their wont) but of reading back into the story an element which is foreign to it.

out-and-out opportunistic capitalist, yet continues to think he can avoid being involved in the same game and so he buries his head (as well as the money) in the sand. Is it not this attitude that makes his fate so inevitable? As soon as his boss realizes that he has no stomach for the risk business he will, of course, get the sack. The fact that he is an honest, law-abiding individual only makes his fate more piquant.[11]

Clearly this is a story about *risk-taking*, its thrust being that the servant cannot hope to live free of risks when a high-flying capitalist has employed him to look after his affairs.

How might the parable have been used? We know that one of Jesus' favourite themes was the need for servants of the Gospel *to dare to* (Mk 10.29; Mt. 10.16; 13.45; Lk. 17.33, among others). I suggest that in this parable Jesus was challenging a disciple who imagined he could avoid the risks involved in being committed to the gospel, pretending to himself that he could get by simply by obeying the rules.

Analogy:	As the agent of a dedicated money-making master is obliged to take risks with his boss's money if he wishes to keep his job	So, seeing that God too is a demanding, opportunistic master would you not be well advised to risk everything he has given you?[12]

Labelling the Characters

Some modern commentators, in struggling to give meaning to the parables, continue this moralizing tendency by giving labels to the various characters in the stories.

The Rich Man and Lazarus (Pb. 55)

Jeremias points out that Jesus based this parable on the conclusion of the popular story about a tax-gatherer Bar Ma'jan and a poor scholar. Bar Ma'jan was a worthless fellow, who had only done one good deed in his entire life: He had arranged a banquet for the city councillors but they never came. As a result, he gave orders that the poor should be invited

11. Some people believe this story justifies capitalism. However, it no more justifies capitalism than the parable of The Indestructible Steward (Pb. 54) justifies fraud. What it commends is a characteristic commonly found in capitalists—a willingness to take risks.

12. The equivalences drawn out in this analogy are justified by the story and in no way represent symbolic representations.

in their stead so that the food should not be wasted. It was the last act of his life, for Bar Ma'jan then suddenly died. He was given a splendid funeral; work stopped throughout the city, since the whole population wished to escort him to his last resting place. At the same time the poor scholar died but no one took any notice of his burial. A few days later in someone's dream the poor scholar was seen walking 'in gardens of paradisal beauty, watered by a flowing stream'. Bar Ma'jan was also seen, standing on the bank of a stream and trying, to no avail, to reach the water.[13]

Jeremias takes the parable as Jesus' response to certain rich and worldly people who refused to take his warning message seriously because they did not believe in a life after death. They were constantly demanding proof of the after-life and the parable is Jesus' reply that none would be given because even if he gave them a sign they would find it meaningless.[14]

Such an interpretation depends on an important inference: The rich man and his five brothers were among those who doubted that there was a life after death. As Jeremias does not explain how he comes to this conclusion we are left to guess that, as Manson claimed,[15] from the clothes the rich man wears hearers would have concluded that he was one of the Sadducees, those arch-conservatives who rejected belief in resurrection.

Personally I find the notion that the man was a Sadducee rather attractive. The description of a wealthy man, who has maintained all his life that death is the end, suddenly waking up to find himself in hell, fits the jokey nature of the story. However, it is one thing to employ such an inference to make a humorous aside and quite another to use it as the premise from which the whole logic of the story flows. We can be very sure that, had Jesus intended his story to be seen as a portrayal of the theological obstinacy of the Sadducees, he would not have left his hearers to surmise it from the description he gave of the man's clothes.

In any case it is, in my view, a mistake to claim that this parable is about belief in an after-life. If the surviving brothers' disbelief in the resurrection was an obstacle to their reform, then Lazarus' miraculous

---

13. G. Dalman as quoted by Jeremias, *Parables*, p. 183. For the various sources of the Bar Ma'jan story and its relevance to Jesus' parables see R. Bauckham, *The Rich Man and Lazarus*, NTS 37.2 (April 1991).

14. Jeremias, *Parables*, pp. 186-87.

15. T.W. Manson, *The Sayings of Jesus*, (London: SCM Press, 1949), p. 296.

appearance from the dead would at least have been pertinent—even if, like Jeremias, one suspects it might not have been sufficient in itself to make them change their ways. On the other hand, 'Moses and the prophets' would have been perfectly useless, seeing that they remain, one and all, silent as the dead on the matter!

To make his interpretation work Jeremias has also to label the rich man and his five brothers 'impious revellers' living in 'selfish luxury'. He is honest enough to admit a 'lack of emphasis on the rich man's guilt' in the story. However he still persists in believing that, to suffer such a fate, the rich man must have been guilty of something more than just being rich. He supports this by arguing that people, knowing that Jesus was drawing on the Bar Maj'an story, would have taken it for granted that the rich man was a sinner. But this argument does not hold up under scrutiny for had people been aware that Jesus was drawing on the Bar Maj'an story they would have taken the rich man to be a publican, not a Sadducee; in which case who knows what his views would have been about the after-life?

Likewise Jeremias is obliged to label Lazarus as pious and humble. In his efforts to prove that the other character in the story was more than just a poor beggar, Jeremias latches on to his name which means 'God helps'. He believes this would have been enough to suggest to Jesus' hearers that the man was both pious and humble; a point he backs up by again appealing to the fact that they would have been aware of the underlying folk-material.

However, I am no more convinced by these arguments than by those for the rich man's guilt. Although the poor man's name and his fate show unmistakably that God is on his side, this tells us nothing about his personal moral state. As regards the underlying folk-material, had people been influenced by it they would have taken Lazarus to be a poor scholar—for that was what he was in the Bar Maj'an story—and this would hardly have confirmed that he was pious.

Jeremias finally convinces me that he is barking up the wrong tree by seeing a need to rewrite Abraham's speech. What Abraham actually says is: 'Son, remember that you in your lifetime received your good things, and Lazarus in like manner evil things; but now he is comforted here, and you are in anguish'. However, Jeremias is at pains to explain that what Abraham actually meant was 'impiety and lovelessness are punished, and piety and humility are rewarded'.[16] I cannot help feeling

16. Jeremias, *Parables*, p. 185.

that the parable's impact would have been dramatically reduced had Jesus' listeners been forced to struggle as hard as Jeremias to squeeze out this point.

Trying to make sense of the story by disparaging the character of the rich man and sanctifying that of Lazarus involves Jeremias in a classical interpretive error. Jesus did not construct the thrusts of his stories by using the gauche device of labelling the characters. He developed them simply from the logic of the situation, which of course is the secret of their effectiveness. In this story it is clear that in his rich man Jesus wishes people to see a rich man behaving as rich men do. Likewise in Lazarus he paints the picture of a poor man being just that.

One further point: The story, in itself, should not be taken too seriously. For example it is naive for Jeremias to argue as he does that the gulf separating heaven and hell 'expresses the irrevocability of God's judgment' and shows that 'Jesus knows no doctrine of purgatory'.[17] In expressing such a view he shows an inability to distinguish between the parable's lighthearted approach, and its deadly serious thrust. The Bar Maj'an story was a popular tale involving an essentially comic reversal of fortunes and people would have expected it to be used with a touch of humour.

How does the story work? In its first part it presents the reversal of the two men's fortunes. As Abraham explains, Lazarus was poor in life so is given joy in Paradise (i.e. meets with God's approval) whereas the other man was rich in life so now suffers Hell (i.e. meets with God's disapproval).

Jeremias claims that to understand the story as simply saying 'on earth, wealth, in the life beyond, torment; on earth, poverty, in the next life, refreshment' cannot be correct for 'Where', he asks, 'has Jesus ever suggested that wealth in itself merits hell, and that poverty in itself is rewarded by paradise?'.[18] If we take paradise as signifying God's

17. Jeremias, *Parables*, pp. 185-86. The best way of judging the role of any component in a parable is to imagine how things would have looked had it not featured. Without the presence of this unsurmountable obstacle people might reasonably have supposed that, since the Law demanded of the rich man that he show solidarity with his brother when he was in need, likewise Lazarus should feel equally bound to help him in his hour of need. This would have ruined the story, which has to make the point that what happens after death is not a continuation of, but a judgment on, what happens in life. In my opinion no more should be made of the 'chasm' than that.

18. Jeremias, *Parables*, p. 185.

approval and hell as signifying God's disapproval—as I am certain we should, for rarely in the synoptic tradition does Jesus show any interest in what happens after death—then the answer is: almost every time he mentions either money or riches.

> You cannot serve God and mammon (Mt. 6.24).

> It is harder for a camel to go through the eye of a needle than for a rich man to enter the kingdom of God (Mk 10.25).

> Blessed are you poor, for yours is the kingdom of God (Lk. 6.20).

> But woe to you that are rich, for you have received your consolation (Lk. 6.24).

In these last two sayings, from the Sermon on the Plain, Jesus does not say 'Blessed are you deserving poor' or 'Woe to you selfish rich'. Does this mean he thought the poor were innately pious and the rich innately loveless? Of course not. No more does this story imply that the poor are always good and the rich always bad. All it suggests is that if you are rich while others are poor then you should not expect to find God with you, to be in his kingdom—or if you want to put it in terms of the after-life mythology: You should not expect to go to heaven.

The biblical tradition (Moses and the prophets) shows a clear aware-ness that as far as Israel was concerned poverty came into existence with the settlement of the tribes in Canaan. It is careful to explain that while poverty would inevitably rear its head in such a settled society (Deut. 15.11), there was nonetheless no excuse for its presence in Israel (Deut. 15.4-5). Which is why, when Israel developed a society with extremes of want and wealth in the eighth century BCE, the prophets condemned people for breaking the Covenant and pointed them back to the pre-settlement days when there was no such distinction. So, as far as the tradition was concerned, the presence of rich and poor side by side in Israel was an affront to God (regardless of individual morality) and was fundamentally condemned as such.

This is exactly the position described in Jesus' story, in which no interest whatsoever is shown in the personal morality of either the rich man or Lazarus. Using the picturesque scene of the afterlife Jesus simply restates the judgment of Moses and the prophets on the rich. Being con-tent with their fortune in a society where others are in want, they bring God's condemnation on themselves because he is the God who favours the poor.

However, I agree with Jeremias that it is not on this first part of the story that attention is focused but on what happens when the rich man asks Abraham to send Lazarus to warn his five brothers. It is here that we first become aware of the common experience around which the story revolves: *the word that carries conviction.*

The rich man is anxious to open his brothers' eyes to this reality he now sees. He believes that a message carried by a resurrected Lazarus (they did not believe in ghosts) will be just the sort of word to carry conviction. The thrust of the story, put once again into the mouth of Abraham, is that such an idea is ludicrous for if the five brothers are not convinced by the tradition itself that being rich puts you in opposition to God then there is no chance that they will be converted by such a miracle.

How might Jesus have used this parable? The story's basic concern is not to get the rich to face up to their position but to get someone else to see the futility of believing that the rich can be 'brought round' by signs and wonders. Perhaps a disciple naively suggested that since Jesus possessed such extraordinary powers and eloquence he should use them to persuade the rich to give up their possessions.

Analogy:	As the five brothers would not have been convinced by a message carried by someone resurrected from the dead	So, is it likely that the rich and powerful will be be persuaded by anything I say or do, however spectacular?

Twinning

Another way in which the evangelists frequently falsify 'the logic of the story' is in treating certain parables as twins or even triplets, thereby transferring aspects of one story to another without warrant.

The Lost Sheep (Pb. 26) and The Lost Coin (Pb. 52)

It is all too easy to transfer to The Lost Sheep aspects that only properly belong to its so-called twin, The Lost Coin. For example Dodd speaks of the 'extravagant concern' shown by the shepherd for the 'trifling' matter of one lost sheep. However, no one would have thought the behaviour of the shepherd extravagant, and the loss of one sheep, even from a flock of a hundred, would never have been considered a small matter. These ideas originate in Luke's companion parable of the lost coin and are out of place in this story.

Again, Dodd and Jeremias take as original to The Lost Sheep the element of rejoicing present in Matthew and Luke (but absent in Thomas). However, it seems probable that this was introduced by the evangelists in order to make the parable conform to their interpretation: God's enthusiastic welcome of the repentant sinner. Notice that while Matthew is fairly restrained in this respect, Luke gets rather carried away. While it would be natural for a shepherd to be pleased at finding his animal, and for his fellow shepherds to congratulate him, none of them would have made a song and dance about something that was all part of the job. Having said this, the main reason for believing that the element of rejoicing was a later addition is that it distracts attention from the story's common experience—that *problem cases call for special treatment*.

To appreciate the thrust of the story of The Lost Sheep one must remember that the relationship of a shepherd to his animals is that they are his livelihood. What the story maintains is that, for a shepherd, good management dictates that after he has left the rest of his flock in a safe place,[19] he must concentrate his attention on the sheep that is lost.

Some may find this hard to take because it goes against the traditional interpretation: love triumphing over all vicissitudes (a sentimental understanding of the economic relationship between the shepherd and his sheep). So here is the story in a form which modern, urban people may more easily appreciate:

> There was once a building contractor who was in charge of five sites. He visited them every day to deal with difficulties as they occurred. However, there came a time when one of them hit big problems. What did he do? Well of course he did what any other manager would: he left the other four sites under the control of their site-foremen and spent the whole week down at the one where everything was going wrong. Indeed, he only returned to the others when he was quite satisfied that everything was, once again, running smoothly.

Clearly, the thrust of this story is the contractor's sound managerial sense in temporarily abandoning the four sites in order to concentrate on the one that has serious problems.[20] Doubtless the building contractor

19. Jeremias, *Parables*, p. 133.

20. A comparable thrust is achieved by Rabbi Judah in his parable of The Twelve Kine: 'A driver had charge of twelve kine laden with wine; when one of them entered the shop of an idolator, the driver left the eleven and followed after the one. Then said they to him, "Why dost thou leave the eleven and follow after the one?" And he replied: "These are in the open street, and I have no fear that the wine will become ritually unfit for use."' (Feldman, *Rabbis*, p. 148).

would have been pleased when he eventually got the problem site back into shape, and certainly his site supervisors would have congratulated him on doing so. However, all this is quite incidental to the story, the impact of which is much greater without intruding this additional element.

If the idea of rejoicing was not original to the story, why did the tradition write it in? Well, although we sometimes forget it, rejoicing was a central element of the parousia message; as central, indeed, as that of judgment. That is why, in Jesus's parables as reported by the evangelists, meals and harvests tend to take on a festive air. So, as the idea of rejoicing went well enough with the story, the early church included it, to make the parable refer to this favourite theme.

Although neither the idea of extravagant concern nor that of rejoicing fit the parable of The Lost Sheep, which is all about the provision of occasional special treatment, they are perfectly applicable to the story of The Lost Coin. It is a common experience to us all that *when we lose a personal possession it suddenly becomes very precious*—much more so than before we lost it. We exteriorize this amplification of our feelings by behaving extravagantly, first displaying a quite unusual concern for what is lost, then giving wild displays of joy and relief when we find it.

So the thrust of this story is that you can only appreciate the woman's extravagant behaviour by seeing it in the light of her loss. How might Jesus have used these parables? Luke was probably right to link them both with the accusation that Jesus was associating too freely with sinners. But perhaps I can be a little more specific: The story of The Lost Sheep concerns the proper role of management in a time of crisis. So maybe we should envisage a group of honest well-wishers chiding Jesus for abandoning them in order to go off and devote himself, for what seemed like an inordinate length of time, entirely to the needs of some worthless individual who had quite needlessly got himself into an impossible scrape.

| Analogy: | As it makes economic sense for the shepherd to leave his flock and give himself entirely to the business of rescuing the animal who has great need of him. | So, does it not make sense, in terms of the kingdom, to respond to the need of someone in great difficulty even though it should mean temporarily abandoning the others? |

In the case of The Lost Coin, I suggest that Jesus' critics were mocking him for the inordinate amount of time and effort he expended on searching out people of apparently little account, and for his disproportionate expressions of joy at their smallest responses.

Analogy:	As the woman is extravagantly concerned when she loses her drachma, and extravagantly happy when she finds it	So, should I not be unusually concerned about people who are lost, and inordinately joyful when they react?

The Need for Lateral Thinking

In dealing with the problem of reconstructing isolated parable stories I have spoken of the need to use one's imagination (lateral thinking) when striving to hit on a viable hypothetical subject for the parable story to illustrate.[21] If this is not done the temptation to devise some way of reconstructing the forgotten subject matter directly out of the parable story will prove too great and the vital gap between the two, the necessary pre-requisite for the parable's proper functioning, will not have been achieved. The following parable illustrates this feature.

The Eye (Pb. 17)

Jeremias describes this logion as a metaphor.[22] However, while it is perfectly true that it *contains* a metaphor, the eye is the lamp, the parable does not depend on it and one can easily rephrase the story leaving it out altogether:

> The eye is the organ that brings light into the body. So if the eye
> is sound, all the other organs are filled with light...

Indeed, had Palestinian houses not been windowless one can well imagine Jesus substituting window for lamp—the former is undoubtedly the more effective way of illuminating a room. We today certainly see it as a better illustration. Properly understood the sole purpose of the metaphor is to direct our attention to the 'light-bringing' function of the eye. Having made this clear the parable goes on to achieve its thrust quite independently.

Matthew in his postscript makes the point that if the inner light in you is corrupted then your soul is indeed in darkness. This is a misleading

21. See pp. 101-102 above.
22. Jeremias, *Parables*, p. 95.

piece of editorial work, since it draws attention away from the story's concern with 'soundness'.

Both evangelists try to make sense of the story by allegorizing its contents rather than by seeing it as a parable addressing some lost incident. In other words, instead of braving the need to make an imaginative (hermeneutical) leap, they develop meaning from the story itself in a linear fashion. They present it as a straightforward teaching to the effect that one should make sure, at all costs, to retain one's spiritual (inner) light. This is an unsatisfactory interpretation on two counts: First, as I have said, attention is drawn to the presence or absence of the light, rather than to the soundness or otherwise of the organ that transmits it; and secondly, the saying is seen as a vehicle for delivering an enigmatic teaching, rather than as a speech-form designed to provoke awareness.

I suggest setting aside the evangelists' interpretations and sticking with the story—which is all about the eye in relation to the rest of the body. Jesus here reminds his listeners of the key role the eye plays in the body—if it is not sound, the whole body will suffer. Accordingly, the common experience upon which the story is built is that of the *crucial role*, the thrust being that if the eye is diseased then the whole body will become blind.

It is with the indispensable aid of this thrust that one has to make the hermeneutical leap. The idea of the eye illuminating the body strongly suggests to me the way in which spiritual and ideological leaders bring, or should bring, understanding to the communities they serve. Perhaps some secret admirer of the Pharisees had become upset by the way Jesus repeatedly denounced their attitudes and behaviour—out of all proportion, as he or she saw it, to their actual sin—and felt moved to ask him why he deemed it necessary to attack them so vigorously. It is important for us to remember that the Pharisees were generally greatly respected. Could it be that Jesus used this parable as a means of getting such a critic to see that leaders who are ideologically unsound need to be watched precisely because, through their influential positions, they adversely affect the whole community?

Analogy:	As the eye has a key position in that the way it functions affects the whole body	So, will not the Pharisees, in occupying key positions within society, also infect everyone else with their exclusive and narrow vision of life?

Compaction

There are several types of parable that one might feel warrant illustration but for the limitation of space.[23] However, one especially deserves attention since it has gone all but unnoticed in previous works: the compacted parable.

Treasure from the Storehouse (Pb. 65)

The import of this saying is that the things we say are important, because others take our words as the measure of our thoughts and therefore of the kind of people we are. This effect is achieved through an analogy in which a person's words are likened to the goods taken from a store and displayed outside in the street to attract customers.

However, because this is a compacted parable it is not easy to draw a clear distinction between the 'story' and 'application' sides of the analogy. One story element—the treasure—has been combined with one application element—the man. The rest remain general; and several—trader, display, store, words, thought, heart—have been dropped altogether.[24] The fact that each evangelist transmits the saying by selecting different elements is an added complication.

On separating out the elements and 'completing' the saying by reinstating those that have been dropped, we are left with the following:

| As the treasure that a trader brings out and displays reveals the quality of what remains in his store (and thus of his whole enterprise) | So, people's words reveal the quality of the thoughts in their hearts (and thus of the people themselves). |

The common experience upon which this analogy is built is *display*; as pertinent now as it must have been in Jesus' day. We naturally judge a shop by the quality of the stock on show in the window when we pass by. If we like what we see we enter and investigate further. The same was true in first-century Palestine, except that for people then it was not a case of looking into the shop window and then going in to buy, but of wandering along looking at the wares laid out on the side of the street and then getting the store-keeper to bring out more merchandise if they liked the look of it. The thrust of the story is therefore that the store-keeper chooses his display from his best goods.

The same applies, Jesus says, to the things a person says. These are

23. See p. 67 above.
24. See possibilities provided by compaction, p. 56 above.

not without consequence, as the speaker may erroneously suppose, for listeners naturally take them as representing the kind of thoughts the speaker has in his or her heart and thus the kind of person he or she is. As Matthew puts it, we will be condemned or justified by the things we say (though, of course, he was probably thinking of the Last Judgment which really has no place in this teaching).

But is it not rather bold to suggest that the underlying analogy is to a storekeeper's display, since no mention is made either of a store or a display in any of the three versions of the saying? And does not the idea of treasure (present in Matthew and Luke, but absent in Thomas) bring more to mind the kind of precious objects any individual might collect, such as a fine jewel or an especially good bottle of wine, and does this not suggest that what we are dealing with here is a private individual's store?

The problem with seeing the analogy as being about a private individual's possessions is that it makes for a much weaker thrust. After all, what is it to me if someone has a marvellous collection of gems or wine? On the other hand, if I am out to buy the stuff, it becomes a matter of considerable importance. As I see it, what we have here, as with so many of Jesus' parables, is a story in which the economics of the situation provides the punch. This also means that the moralistic element that the evangelists have introduced by talking about good and bad people is quite out of place. What the story is concerned with is simply a common sense practice to draw customers.

Analogy:	As the objects the trader brings out to display are taken as a sign of the quality of the goods he has in his store	So, is it not foolish to allow yourself to say crass things for they will inevitably be taken as a manifestation of the kind of person you are?

Chapter 8

PARABLES PRESENTING SPECIAL CHALLENGES

Can Allegorization always be Avoided?

For reconstructionists, the parable of The Rebellious Tenants poses a very particular problem for, as Drury so rightly remarks, 'Exegete after exegete has found it impossible to understand it in any other way' than as an allegory.[1]

The Rebellious Tenants (Pb. 13)
Jeremias investigates the allegorization of the parable in detail. He starts by noting how its opening has been altered to echo Isaiah's song of the vineyard (5.1-7). He goes on to describe how Mark and Matthew have each in his own way made the servants symbolize the prophets. He shows that Matthew and Luke have had the son cast out of the vineyard before he is murdered in order to refer to Jesus' death outside the city walls. Finally he points out that the saying about the rejected stone has been added to predict the resurrection.

In spite of this, Jeremias still maintains that Jesus meant his hearers to understand that the vineyard = Israel, that he himself should be identified as the son, and that the story was a prediction that the Jewish authorities would be ousted. Indeed the only symbolic element in the evangelists' extended allegory which both he and Dodd reject is the servants = prophets equation. Yet both of them strenuously deny that their interpretations are allegorical.[2]

But as Drury has pointed out this is not good enough. Either we must accept that the story of The Rebellious Tenants is a reformulation of Isaiah's allegory of the vineyard and therefore not a parable at all, in my terms, or we must reject all representations within it. I believe the story

---

1. Drury, *Parables*, p. 64.
2. Jeremias, *Parables*, p. 76; Dodd, *Kingdom*, p. 98.

was a parable. So I have to put my trust in its teller, concentrating solely on the logic he gave it, unpalatable as this may be.

Jesus' story reflects the nationalist peasant/absentee landlord situation in Galilee. Dodd reminds us that large estates in Palestine were held by foreigners and that this would have been a point of resentment for the local people, who had never really given up the nationalist struggle resurrected by Judas the Gaulonite in 6 CE.[3]

The pattern of most tenant/landlord disputes is a kind of poker game to decide who has the strongest nerve. Technically, the last word lies with the law. However, if it is to be enforced, everything hinges on whether the injured party is prepared to stand up and exercise his or her will by taking the matter to court. Today, if the landlord is a timid old lady, the tenants may well feel that they can disregard her—until a letter from her lawyer appears on the doormat!

In this particular story the tenants have one advantage: the landlord is absent. As long as he operates from a distance he is only a threat. The tenants are effectively in charge on the ground, as they prove by meting out their own justice upon successive rent-collectors. Only the local authorities have the power of coercion, so everything depends on the landlord taking up his case with them in person. In the story, one senses this weakness in the landlord's position.

So why does he not make the journey sooner? Perhaps he feels he has more important things to do. We should bear in mind how protracted and dangerous long journeys were in those days. If we take into account the stories of people being robbed, shipwrecked, or for other reasons dying on the way, it is not difficult to imagine the landlord hesitating to make such a journey and the tenants taking advantage of this fact.

Indeed, the tenants' actions up to the murder have an air of well- calculated risk. It is only when they kill the landlord's son that we sense a corner has been turned. From this moment on we know their game is up. Now the landlord is bound to attempt the hazardous journey and—if he makes it—the tenants are doomed.

To properly understand the thrust of the story we must now try to determine the reasons for the tenants' crazy action. It occurred to me that they might have revolted because the landlord was exploiting them. Tenant farmers have often historically become rebellious because they

3. Dodd, *Kingdom*, p. 94.

have felt oppressed. However, there are problems with this interpretation. If Jesus had meant the story to be taken in this way he would have made it clear that the owner was a bad landlord. This he does not do. Indeed, according to Thomas the landlord is a 'good' man (although admittedly no undue weight should be attached to this: It was probably added to clear God of the stigma attached to absentee-landlords).

Having abandoned this workers' view of the story I was tempted to understand the tenants' motivation by seeing them as greedy. This would be the management view of the story (the one most commentators take). However, although it cannot be denied that the tenants betray a distorted attitude, it is as simplistic to explain their actions by saying they were greedy as it is to justify their actions by saying that the landlord is bad. I think the truth is that in keeping with his other parables Jesus was simply describing types of people as he found them. Thus he draws a picture of an absentee landlord behaving in the way an absentee landlord would. The man is neither good nor bad, just an absentee landlord. This is one of the characteristic strengths of Jesus' story-telling. He does not make his point by labelling his characters 'good', 'bad' or anything else, but allows them to be seen for what they are through the natural working out of the story.

So let us forget about labels and, instead, ask ourselves what it is about being a tenant that puts people on edge. Once this question is asked everything falls into place. What many of us find intolerable about the position of tenant is that although we are happy to have the use of a piece of property we feel uneasy when we do not *own* it. There is something very strong within us that tells us that only when something is finally ours will we be freed from the disagreeable sensation of being dependent on someone else, of being as it were juvenile and not altogether responsible. In short, as much as we find the position of owner self-enhancing, we find the position of tenant demeaning. People on a mortgage will understand this. They long for the day when the house is paid up, not just because it will make their financial situation easier but because the house will then be well and truly theirs.

As I see it, what really upset those tenants when they saw the rent collector arriving, was not that they would have to give up some of their hard-earned produce, but that his presence reminded them that they did not own the vineyard and were dependent for their livelihood on their landlord's good will. In their own eyes they were belittled by their position. So, when they murdered the heir it was not because they were greedy and wanted to have all the produce for themselves, but because it was the only way they could see themselves gaining possession.

Desire for ownership is the common experience at the heart of this story, the thrust being generated by the way in which the tenants' overweening desire for possession drives them to commit the ultimate folly.

In what circumstances might Jesus have used this parable? The evangelists all claim he was targeting the Temple authorities and I can find no good reason to disagree with them. We know that some of the Temple priests took an active part in the disastrous Jewish revolt some forty years later. So could it be that one of them had expressed the opinion that God had destined the Sadducees, not the Romans, to be the masters in Israel and the parable was Jesus' reply?

Analogy	As the tenants, dominated by their desire to own the vineyard, were led to commit a disastrous act of folly	So, in your lust for 'ownership' of Israel and your frustration with Roman domination, are you Sadducees not in danger of calling down disaster upon yourselves?

Exemplary Stories?

Though it may not be too difficult to accept, in theory, the notion that Jesus would not have used exemplary stories involving fictitious characters,[4] it is quite another matter to accept this postulate in practice, especially when Jesus is reported as terminating one of his parables by telling his interlocutor to 'go and do likewise', as was the case in the following parable.

The Samaritan (Pb. 44)

Jeremias argues that the introductory discussion between the lawyer and Jesus on the subject of the two great commandments should not be taken as Luke's version of the conversation on the same subject reported in Mark (12.28-34) and Matthew (22.34-40).

It is worth noting that although Mark and Matthew have certainly recorded the same conversation their accounts differ from one another in one fundamental respect. Matthew writes that the discussion was the consequence of a group of Pharisees 'testing' Jesus to see if they could

---

4.   See p. 41 above.

trip him up and make him appear fallible after hearing how he had silenced their theological rivals, the Sadducees. Matthew opens his account with the question 'What is the great commandment?' being put to Jesus by one of the Pharisees, and ends by describing how Jesus routed his opponents by asking a testing question of his own. Mark presents the discussion in a very different light. Although he opens with the same question, he says that the scribe who posed it did so because he was impressed by how well Jesus had answered the Sadducees; and he ends his account not with the man being put to shame but with Jesus telling him that he is not far from the kingdom.

Jeremias argues that, like Mark's scribe, Luke's theologian was well intentioned. He had probably been affected by Jesus' preaching and, in answering his question about what was written in the Law, may have been quoting Jesus himself. Jeremias denies the sting in the phrase 'wishing to justify himself', claiming that the man was indeed justified in asking the supplementary question 'Who is my neighbour?', for it was a subject of some dispute.[5]

But what Luke says is that the lawyer 'stood up to put Jesus to the test' and, as we have seen from Matthew, such a formula normally indicates hostility. The natural reading of Luke's version is that the theologian was perfectly aware Jesus could only answer his question by taking sides in a fractious structural dispute; a situation he knew Jesus was characteristically careful to avoid.[6]

The interesting feature of Luke's account is that Jesus does not answer the question about who falls into the category 'neighbour'. His response concerns people who act or do not act as neighbour, which is not the same issue. The natural way of understanding Luke here is that Jesus was intentionally avoiding the trap which the theologian had set for him by giving the questioner an ideological response to his structural question. Manson makes the point felicitously in his own way:

> No definition of 'neighbour' emerges from the parable: and for a very good reason. The question is unanswerable, and ought not to be asked. For love does not begin by defining its objects: it discovers them.[7]

5.   Jeremias, *Parables*, pp. 202-203.

6.   See for example the controversies about divorce, Mk 10.2-9; and taxes, Mk 12.13-14.

7.   Manson, *Sayings*, p. 261.

Jeremias, however, sees things differently. For him this apparent gap between the lawyer's question and Jesus' answer is merely a formal inconsistency:

> The alteration in the form of the question hardly conceals a deeper meaning. It is simply a formal inconsistency in which there is nothing surprising when once the philological facts are realized: the word *reᶜa* (neighbour) implies a reciprocal relation, like our word 'comrade'. When a man calls anyone his comrade, he assumes the responsibility to treat him as a comrade. Thus both Jesus and the scribe are after the same thing: they are not seeking a definition, but the extent of the conception *reᶜa*.[8]

But this will not do. Swapping 'friend' or 'neighbour' for 'comrade' changes nothing. The reply to 'Who acted as a comrade in my story?' is still no answer to 'Who should I consider as my comrade?' Of course, Jeremias is right to note that the scribe was looking for an indication of the extent of the conception *reᶜa*. Jesus, however, was not. By refusing to reply in the terms dictated by the question, he showed that he was consistent in his refusal to be drawn into structural debates.

As I see it, Jeremias's hypothesis—that the theologian was well intentioned—is at variance with everything Luke writes. This is an important issue, for either there was nothing wrong with the theologian's attitude—in which case Jesus was simply attempting to make him aware of something that was new to him—or else there was, and Jesus was attempting to deal with this basic fault.

Jeremias sees the parable as Jesus' way of enabling the scribe 'to measure the absolute and unlimited nature of the duty of love'[9] and 'to teach him that no human being was beyond the range of his charity'.[10] He makes the following points about the way in which the story functions:

1.   The parable has the effect of changing the point of view of the observer by getting him to put himself in the sufferer's place.[11] Is there any real evidence that Jesus intended this effect? A modern writer desiring to direct her or his readers' attention in this way would simply recount what took place from the victim's point of view. The writer would describe how the man lay in a stupor in the road, listening to the footsteps of those who passed by, wondering why they never came to

8.   Jeremias, *Parables*, p. 205.
9.   Jeremias, *Parables*, p. 204.
10.   Jeremias, *Parables*, p. 205.
11.   Jeremias, *Parables*, p. 205.

his aid. While such a psychological approach was not available to Jesus, had he been trying to get the scribe to see things through the eyes of the sufferer he would surely have given the latter a name. As it is, he tells his story in such a way that the man who fell among thieves is the only character who is not given an identity and who remains entirely passive throughout, his role being simply to get beaten up.[12]

2. The parable works in such a way as to introduce a shift from theory to practice.[13] Jeremias is right to say that the theologian is looking at things from a theoretical point of view but Jesus would surely have found nothing intrinsically wrong in that—had the man's theory been soundly based. Then again, while it would have been reasonable to take the Samaritan's actions as a practical example of good-neighbourly behaviour (had it been acceptable to build such a model on a fictitious character, which I do not believe it was) little would have been achieved by so doing since Jesus' interlocutor would have known well enough what being a good neighbour entailed. Jesus was not giving this theologian a moral lesson, he was calling out of him something he instinctively knew already, to oblige him to bring it to bear on the real issue between them.

If I am right in thinking that the precise circumstances (incidents) which led to Jesus telling his parables were, almost without exception, forgotten before they could be recorded, it is not unreasonable to suppose that if, in this instance, anything had survived it would have been some vague memory of a clash between Jesus and the religious establishment over the neighbour question. This would explain why Luke introduced the parable by saying that a theologian intended to test Jesus.

Given such a point of departure, Luke's problem would have been how to introduce the 'Who is my neighbour?' question into a hypothetical conversation. If Jeremias is right in saying that Jesus often summarized the Law in the two commandmants, 'Love God' and 'Love your neighbour', then a discussion about the Law would naturally have suggested itself as a suitable starting point. Maybe Luke already had an account of such a conversation in his possession; perhaps even the same as that recorded in Mark and Matthew. In any case, he has the theologian commence by asking a question about eternal life, whereupon Jesus

12. The figure of Abel plays a similar role in the Genesis story (4.1-16). His name, meaning 'ephemeral', indicates that he too has no other part to play but that of victim, murdered by his brother Cain.

13. Jeremias, *Parables*, p. 205.

refers him to the Law. Now he is able to have the scribe bring out his question about the neighbour, hoping to embarrass Jesus by embroiling him in an argument about religious structures. The range of people a good Jew was required to treat as his brothers was a particularly thorny issue of the day.

I do not wish to appear over-confident about these deductions. I am simply exploring the possible ways in which the early church's editors may have operated. Of course the actual process is beyond recovery. However, this much is clear: They were working from, at best, imprecise memories of the original incidents and, at worst, no memories at all.

Bearing this in mind, we should not be too concerned that Luke's reconstructed conversation seems slightly artificial. It is enough to know that here we have a confrontation between Jesus and a learned theologian, over a much discussed and hotly debated structural issue. Of course we have no way of knowing what the man's personal opinion on the question was. All we can say for sure is that he thought it could and should be asked and answered.

Jeremias describes the various arguments adduced in this debate:

> It was generally agreed that the term [*re^ca* = neighbour] connoted fellow-countrymen, including full proselytes, but there was disagreement about the exceptions; The Pharisees were inclined to exclude non-Pharisees; the Essenes required that a man 'should hate all the sons of darkness'; a rabbinical saying ruled that heretics, informers, and renegades 'should be pushed (into a ditch) and not pulled out', and a wide-spread popular saying excepted personal enemies ('You have heard that God said: You shall love your fellow-countryman; but you need not love your enemy', Mt. 5.43).[14]

However he shows little understanding of the mentality of the debaters. As I see it, their error was to think they could satisfy God by arbitrarily defining the Law's limits for the chosen people and then acting accordingly.

What Jesus showed, through his parable—its common experience—was that as God sees things, *the righteousness of behaviour is determined solely by how people measure up to the material exigencies of the situation in which they find themselves.* In other words it is not a case of the person determining the requirements of the situation by reference to some ideal standard but of the material situation exposing the true nature of the individual's attitude and behaviour.

14. Jeremias, *Parables*, pp. 202-203.

This is perhaps the point Jeremias is striving to make when he accuses the theologian of being theoretical and self-centred. However, as I see it, the theologian's attitude-defect had nothing to do either with the theoretical/practical or selfish/other-centred divides. His 'sin' is rather that of *idealism*. Some intellectuals—like this theologian—habitually avoid the unpleasant business of facing up to reality, by concocting ideas about how things ought to be, and then urging society to follow them. If I am right in thinking that this theologian was guilty of running away from reality and indulging in 'idealistic' pursuits we must see the story as aimed at bringing him down to earth.

Jeremias describes Jesus' choice of characters—on the one hand the priest and Levite and on the other the Samaritan—as 'an extreme example', selected in order to contrast two types of behaviour.[15] However, judged in terms of the neighbour debate it is not so much extreme as typical, the priest and Levite epitomizing the kind of person whom those involved in the great debate would have included as 'neighbours', and the Samaritan the kind of person they would have wanted to exclude.

Thus, in Jesus' story, we are presented with a plausible situation in which the first-class candidates for the position of neighbour don't behave in a neighbourly way, whereas the despised outsider does: its thrust being that *a Jew* is not justified by his scrupulous maintenance of certain limited obligations that define his membership of the chosen people, but by acting as Yahweh expects: in a healthy, life-affirming manner.

In other words the parable's impact serves to expose the whole 'Who is my neighbour?' debate as an idealistic charade and leaves the debaters looking ridiculous. This is how the theologian would have experienced it and it cannot have been pleasant—but then healing processes seldom are.

Critics may say I exaggerate the difference between my position and that of Jeremias since both of us think the parable underlines the importance of loving everyone who comes our way. However, the difference is not here but in the way we see the parable being used. To him, it is an illustrative teaching, given in a relaxed and friendly exchange, which enables the theologian thereafter to properly measure the duty of love. To me, the parable is a searing public exposure of an attitude-defect revealed by those who are involved in the 'Who is my neighbour?'

15. Jeremias, *Parables*, p. 204.

debate; something that would have made the theologian ashamed or else filled him with such rage that he would have gladly joined those who were prepared to crucify Jesus.

Because Christian tradition has, for hundreds of years, interpreted the parable of the Samaritan as an attack on men's and women's selfishness and unwillingness to respond to the needs of others, many people will find my interpretation hard to take. So, to help them experience the parable as I believe it must have been experienced by Jesus' audience, I offer this modern reformulation:

> There was once a politician who frequently voiced the opinion that Britain shouldn't be bothered with the Third World. His claim was that we should have learnt from our colonialist past that outsiders are no good at running other people's countries for them. 'It is folly for us to take responsibility for them' he was heard to say, 'We are manifestly incapable of carrying the burden.' He believed each country should only assume the responsibilities it was able to fulfil, which for him basically meant ensuring the welfare of its own people.

> One day the politician found himself on a radio panel with an elderly lady he did not know but who was there because she had recently been in the news. Never one to miss an opportunity, he turned to her and said 'Madam you seem to me to be a woman who knows her mind. Don't you sometimes feel irritated by these people who are forever claiming that the developed world should bail out countries which have proved incapable of looking after themselves?'

> The elderly lady answered by telling him this story:

> 'A British naval task force was on its way to the Persian gulf when it got into difficulties in the Indian Ocean. I don't remember the details of the incident', she said, 'but they became stranded. The French had ships in the area but they declined to help because they said that they needed approval from the other members of the European Community. The U.S. navy were also in a position to give assistance, but they too declined on the grounds that Great Britain had refused to send them minesweepers when they had needed them. However, the Ethiopian navy, when it heard of the plight of the British sailors, sent off both its ships and brought them all to safety.'

> When the elderly lady had finished her story she turned to the politician and said 'Who do you think acted responsibly?' He, blushing angrily, replied 'Those who helped I suppose'.

> 'Exactly' said the elderly lady 'So, don't you think we should behave as they did?'

Jesus' own formula: 'Go and do likewise', performs exactly the same function as my elderly lady's 'Don't you think we should behave as they did?' Far from indicating that the stories are being used to exemplify the kind of desirable conduct that is being called for, these formulae constitute in fact just the closing of the door of the parabolic trap.[16]

Analogy:	As the first-class neighbours did not act in a neighbourly way whereas the despised outsider did	So, why try to define the limits of your caring if all that matters is to react appropriately when you meet someone in need?

Indefensible Conduct?

One parable presents a formidable challenge to commentators of every persuasion.

The Indestructible Steward (Pb. 54)

Inevitably, every interpretation of this parable is likely to be judged by the way in which it handles the steward's persistent criminality. Jeremias believes that none of the various attempts to exonerate the steward[17] or, alternatively, to use him as 'a dreadful warning'[18] have been successful.

Like the parable of The Banquet (Pb. 27) this is one of Jesus' 'escape-artist' stories whose common experience is *the natural self-love which affirms a person's identity in everything he or she does*. Not surprisingly, therefore, the basic pattern of each story is the same. The central character has offended, and his crime has caught up with him. He is in a trap from which there is apparently no escape. In prospect is his utter humiliation. However, instead of succumbing the 'hero' is galvanized by his self-love and finds a way to an unexpected triumph.

On this level the two stories are identical. However, each establishes its unique character in the way it details the particular avenue of escape dictated by the set-up. In the parable of The Banquet, the tax-collector is looking for social acceptance; so he escapes by finding an alternative and quite unlooked-for solidarity with the outcasts. In this parable, the steward is looking for sheer survival and the story explains how he assures his future by sharing with others the benefits of his crime and so making them beholden to him.

16. See attitude-straightening parables as 'cornering the prey', p. 68 above.
17. Jeremias, *Parables*, p. 182 n. 42.
18. Jeremias, *Parables*, p. 47.

This compounding of the crime—technically achieved by the way in which the steward 'exports' his fraud and spreads its benefits —is, as I see it, essential to the logic of the story of The Indestructible Steward. It is also the feature that makes it, for us who are more or less slaves to morality, devilishly hard to handle. Yet there is no doubt that this feature of the story is responsible for generating the special delight we feel at the steward's escape. We understand instinctively that it would ruin the effect were there to be a legal way for him to extract himself from his predicament. In other words this particular component is not an adjunct to the story, it is the crucial aspect that furnishes the story with its specific character. The fact that the steward is so hemmed in, making it impossible for him to preserve his life otherwise than by compounding his fraud, serves to establish that, *since it is seeking life that counts, giving up and dying because that is what morality dictates would be plain stupid.* This is the thrust of the story.

One of the most characteristic features of Jesus as he is portrayed by the evangelists was his out-and-out refusal to do the usual religious thing and play on his hearers' sense of personal *worthiness*, their altruism and commitment to excellence. His approach, from which he never deviated, was to appeal to peoples' profoundest desire for personal *advantage* (Mt. 5.12; 6.4, 18; Mk 8.35-36; Lk. 6.35-38; 12.31, 33; 18.29 etc.). For him, entrance to the kingdom was not to be obtained by those who blinkered their vision by trusting to moral precepts—the measure by which they judged themselves to be worthy. Rather, it was open to those who approached life with eyes wide open to its opportunities. Accordingly he was always at pains to encourage self-love, as in this parable, since only when motivated by it did a person have any chance at all of responding to the gospel.

It is true that Jesus strongly discriminated between greater and lesser advantages, between those which he described as bringing 'life', seized only by people whom he described as having 'faith' (Mt. 8.10; 15.28; Lk. 7.50; 8.48, for example), and those which become obstacles when given priority, like food, clothing, money, honour and power. However, it was this basic desire in a person for her or his own advantage that Jesus chose to work on and never despised, rather than the desire to achieve standards and to become better, so often the objective which religious people pursue.

How might Jesus have used this parable? Suppose he is one day confronted by a disciple who is an 'old moralist' (We know there were many of these in the early church since we can see their hand in the tradition's editorial work). The man is going on about how lax and degenerate society has become. 'What upsets me most about people these days', he explains to Jesus, 'is how different they are from you and me. Whereas we are strongly motivated by the desire for the life of excellence prescribed in our Law, these people seem only concerned with their petty personal advantage.' Could Jesus have told such a person this story to try to free him from the mental trap he had dug himself into?

Analogy:	As the steward was manifestly right to ensure his continued survival, even though this meant adding considerably to his crimes	So, is it not right for people to champion their lives rather than become the slaves of the community's precepts?

Deformed Past Reconstruction?
The difficulty in reconstructing any parable depends on the extent to which it has been deformed either by the natural process of disintegration with time or by the early church's editorial work.[19] One parable in particular appears to be very damaged, making it a reconstructionist's nightmare.

Sheep and Goats (Pb. 41)
Jeremias sheds light on the story by pointing out that in Palestine it is normal for a shepherd to own a mixed flock and that it is customary for him to separate them in the evening because goats, being more susceptible to the cold, need shelter, whereas sheep prefer the open air.

He has several stabs at finding symbolic references, remarking for instance that in other New Testament writings the gathering of the scattered flock is a feature of the Messianic Age. He justifies the equations: sheep = the righteous, and goats = the cursed, by saying that the superior value of sheep, their white coloration (as opposed to the black of the goats) make them 'a symbol of the righteous'. Finally, he suggests that 'the separation = the final judgment'.[20]

As I see it, the pattern of a gathering followed by a separation would, indeed, have constituted a fine basis for a parable. It is such a simple, powerful juxtaposition that it would have made an impact not easily to

19. See pp. 91-92 above.
20. Jeremias, *Parables*, p. 206.

be forgotten. But if such a pattern was indeed the basis for this particular parable why does the gathering of the flock not figure in the story?

The early church editors tended to link gathering with sorting whenever they could; the harvest being one of their favourite ways of depicting the parousia. So it seems extremely unlikely that, in a story where both elements were originally present they would have subsequently allowed one of them to disappear. The fact that the gathering element is absent from the simile—though not of course from the logion as a whole—is a strong indication that it was not part of the parabolic story in the first place.

Notice also the curious way in which the sheep and goats are fitted into the general judgment story. Even if you happen to think that a shepherd separating his animals is a suitable simile for the way in which God will eventually sort the 'righteous' from the 'cursed' on Judgment Day (which I do not), once the simile has been introduced it makes no sense to further extend its use, as Matthew seems determined to do in v. 33. For while it is perfectly acceptable to speak about the righteous being placed on God's right-hand side (traditionally the place of honour and fortune) and the wicked on his left (traditionally the place of misery), I can think of no satisfactory reason why a shepherd should choose to do the same with his sheep and goats.

Jeremias's contention that the separation constitutes the final judgment means of course that he is happy to read the simile symbolically. However, given the fact that similes are inevitably weakened by the introduction of symbolic references it is fair to assume that the equations sheep = the righteous, and goats = the cursed are editorial allegorizations. I believe they are the result of Matthew's attempt to insert the originally independent sheep/goats simile into the overall judgment logion.

I suggest Matthew's original text ran something like this:

> Before him will be gathered all the nations, and he will separate them one from another. And he will place the righteous at his right hand but the wicked at his left. Then the king will say...

He then inserted Jesus' sheep/goats simile into the middle of it:

> Before him will be gathered all the nations, and he will separate them one from another *as a shepherd separates the sheep from the goats*, and he will place...

But now he was presented with a choice. Should he continue with the sheep/goats simile or revert back to the righteous and wicked formula of his original text? I think he was forced to choose the first option because only by making the symbolism clear could he provide the simile with any real sense:

> ...and he will place the sheep at his right hand, but the goats at his left...

In the present context the simile depends for its effect on the reader clearly identifying sheep as valuable and goats as a nuisance. But while it is true, as Jeremias says, that sheep are more valuable it would be a mistake to suggest that, for the shepherd, goats are an economic liability.

The reason why Palestinian shepherds kept mixed flocks is because goats will graze on plants that sheep will not touch. So, while it is true to say that a sheep will fetch more money than a goat on the open market, the overall value of the flock is much greater when it includes both sorts of animal. Any Palestinian shepherd would have thought Jesus quite mad had he suggested that having goats in one's flock was like having pests. The same argument holds for the suggestion that Jesus might have relied for the thrust of his story on the colour of the animals. Black goat's hair may not be worth as much as white wool but it still has commercial value.

Whichever way you look at it, the separation of sheep from goats is inadequate as a simile for the Last Judgment: There is simply no convincing way of seeing sheep as valuable and goats as harmful. When the prophets wanted a simile to do this job they spoke of threshers separating grain from chaff (Zeph. 2.1-2). Such a simile, associated as it is with the harvest, emphasizes the economic angle, from which perspective some things are clearly desirable and others a nuisance. It is this contrast that best illustrates the distinction between the righteous and the wicked and it is precisely this contrast that the simile of sheep and goats lacks.

So it would seem that Matthew's efforts to save the simile for posterity by integrating it into his judgment logion was misguided for by doing so he succeeded in portraying Jesus as a second-rate communicator who first introduces a meaningless comparison and then covers up his mistake by making out that it should be understood figuratively.

Of course, we who are a thousand miles removed from the economic realities of Palestinian sheep farming and who have been fed from our cradles on Matthew's text, are convinced that the simile somehow works. But the force we experience on reading it is not in fact the impact of the simile but the power of Jesus' dark saying about the last judgment, slightly alleviated by the pastoral figure. This is very different from what Jesus' audience would have felt when in a completely different context, as I believe, he told them his sheep and goats story. They would have experienced a parabolic thrust that threw them back onto their real-life experience of steppeland herding.

Clearly the common experience on which Jesus built his sheep and goats story had something to do with a separation, so everything depends on the reason for this separation. Jeremias maintains that as the word appears in the present tense Jesus must have been citing an habitual practice: the Palestinian shepherds' sorting out the goats from their flocks each evening. If this is the correct interpretation, as seems highly plausible, we are not dealing with an extraction of the harmful from the valuable but rather with *the routine provision of special treatment, on good economic grounds, for animals with special needs.*

How might Jesus have used the story? It is difficult to avoid a comparison with the parable of The Lost Sheep (Pb. 26), which is also about providing special treatment. The principal difference, however, is that while in the story of the lost sheep special treatment is required as a result of an animal getting into difficulties, in this story special treatment is provided on a regular basis.

I have argued that the parable of The Lost Sheep was probably used by Jesus to answer a criticism voiced by some among his disciples that Jesus was always abandoning them to go after some silly person who had got himself into trouble quite unnecessarily.[21] In the case of this parable I think the criticism must have come from some 'high flyer'; from a person who had complained that Jesus seemed to prefer to spend his time with people who were weak by nature and so had little to contribute. If he was serious about bringing in the kingdom he would have to learn to invest himself where his efforts would pay dividends: with people like this critic who were making things happen and getting things done in the community.

Analogy:	As the shepherd finds it to his economic advantage to provide special treatment for those animals with special needs	So, will I not find it profitable, in achieving my ends, if I direct most of my of his attention towards those whose needs are greatest?

21. See p. 139 above.

BIBLIOGRAPHY

Blomberg, C.L., *Interpreting the Parables* (Leicester: Apollos, 1990).

Boucher, M., *The Mysterious Parable* (Washington: Catholic Biblical Association of America, 1977).

Bultmann, R., *The History of the Synoptic Tradition* (Oxford: Basil Blackwell, 1963).

Cadoux, A.T., *The Parables of Jesus: Their Art and Use* (London: J. Clarke, 1930).

Coggin, R.J., and J.L. Houlden (eds.), *A Dictionary of Biblical Interpretation* (London: SCM Press, 1990).

Crossan, J.D., *In Parables: The Challenge of the Historical Jesus* (New York: Harper & Row, 1973).

Drury, J., *The Parables in the Gospels: History and Allegory* (London: SPCK, 1985).

Dodd, C.H., *The Parables of the Kingdom* (London: Collins, rev. edn, 1961).

Feldman, A.F., *The Parables and Similes of the Rabbis* (Cambridge: Cambridge University Press, 1924).

Fuchs, E., *Studies of the Historical Jesus* (London: SCM Press; Nashville: Alec R. Allenson, 1964).

Funk, R.W., *Language, Hermeneutic and the Word of God: The Problem of Language in the New Testament and Contemporary Theology* (New York: Harper & Row, 1966).

Funk, R.W., B.B. Scott and J.R. Butts (eds.), *The Parables of Jesus, Red Letter Edition: The Jesus Seminar* (Sonoma, CA: Polebridge Press, 1988).

Goulder, M.D., *Midrash and Lection in Matthew* (London: SPCK, 1974).

—*The Evangelist's Calendar* (London: SPCK, 1978).

Hedrick, C.W., *Parables as Poetic Fictions: The Creative Voice of Jesus* (Peabody, MA: Hendrickson Publishers, 1995).

Hunter, A.M., *Interpreting the Parables* (London: SCM Press, 1960).

James, M.R., *The Apocryphal New Testament* (Oxford: Clarendon Press, 1924).

Jeremias, J., *The Parables of Jesus* (London: SCM Press, rev. edn, 1972).

Julicher, A., *Die Gleichnisreden Jesu* (Freiburg: Mohr, 1899).

Jungel, E., *Paulus und Jesus* (Tübingen: Mohr, 1962).

Kissinger, W.S., *The Parables of Jesus: A History of Interpretation and Bibliography* (Metuchen, NJ: The Scarecrow Press, 1979).

Linneman, E., *Jesus of the Parables: Introduction and Exposition* (London: SPCK, 1966).

Manson, T.W., *The Teachings of Jesus* (Cambridge: Cambridge University Press, 1939).

—*The Sayings of Jesus* (London: SCM Press, 1949).

Oesterley, W.O.E., *The Gospel Parables in the Light of their Jewish Background* (London: SPCK; New York: Macmillan, 1936).

Perrin, N., *Jesus and the Language of the Kingdom* (London: SCM Press; Philadelphia: Fortress Press, 1976).

Richards, I.A., *Philosophy of Rhetoric* (London: Oxford University Press, 1936)

Ricoeur, P., *The Rule of Metaphor* (Toronto: University of Toronto Press, 1977).

Sanders, E.P., *Jesus and Judaism* (London, SCM Press, 1985).

Scott, B.B., Jesus, *Symbol-Maker of the Kingdom* (Philadelphia: Fortress Press, 1981).

—*Hear Then a Parable: A Commentary on the Parables* (Philadelphia: Fortress Press, 1989).

Soskice, J.M., *Metaphor and Religious Language* (Oxford: Clarendon Press, 1985).

Via, D.O., *The Parables: Their Literary and Existential Dimensions* (Philadelphia: Fortress Press, 1967).

Weder, H., *Die Gleichnisse Jesu als Metaphern* (Göttingen: Vandenhoeck & Ruprecht, 1978).

Wilder, A.N., *The Language of the Gospel: Early Christian Rhetoric* (New York: Harper & Row, 1964).

INDEXES

INDEX OF REFERENCES

OLD TESTAMENT

NEW TESTAMENT

THE BIBLICAL SEMINAR